LIQUID
dessert

LIQUID
dessert

Cocktail Confections from Around the World

Bryan Paiement

RED ⚡ LIGHTNING BOOKS

This book is a publication of

RED ⚡ LIGHTNING BOOKS
1320 East 10th Street
Bloomington, Indiana 47405 USA

redlightningbooks.com

© 2023 by Bryan Paiement

Manufactured in the United States of America

First Printing 2023

Cataloging information is available from
the Library of Congress.

ISBN 978-1-68435-211-1 (hardback)
ISBN 978-1-68435-212-8 (ebook)

Contents

LIQUID
dessert

Introduction

We have all been there before: facing the decision, after a delicious meal, of whether to indulge or not—dessert or no dessert? Many of us, myself included, trend toward having dessert as a culinary closure of sorts. That little bit of sweetness after a meal helps put the finishing touch on what was hopefully a wonderful dining experience.

And this decision is certainly not limited to evenings when you may be dining out. *To dessert or not to dessert* is a ubiquitous theme in our everyday lives, whether you're lounging on the couch, picnicking outside, or picking up drive-through for a hungry family on the move. I'm a bartender at a restaurant in Colorado, and when I approach customers once they have finished their dinner to ask about dessert, they peer at whatever cocktail or wine they happen to be drinking. I see their wheels spinning, because for many, the options are clear: either order another drink or forgo alcohol in favor of a dessert. *Liquid Dessert* solves this dilemma, as the recipes in this collection combine the best of both worlds, melding your favorite dessert flavors and spirits into delicious cocktail confections that will satisfy your sweet tooth and your desire to imbibe and enjoy the company of friends and family.

It was certainly eye-opening to research so many of the world's most beloved desserts and learn the often-fascinating origins behind seemingly simple treats such as carrot cake, cannoli, and éclairs, just to name a few. Whether you're a fan of rich, decadent chocolate or you have more of a citrusy, tart palate, the cocktails in *Liquid Dessert* have you covered. From Canada and Mexico to Africa and even Antarctica, there is no limit to the distance I covered in my research to create cocktails inspired by the best desserts on the planet. This is not your average cocktail or dessert book but a conglomeration of the two.

Liquid Dessert will take you on a journey across the seven continents to explore the most famous desserts different countries have to offer. I then transform these rich delicacies into delectable dessert cocktails. Not only will you love the opportunity to be your own mixologist from the comfort of your home, but you will learn the traditions and origins of desserts from around the world. The history behind the world's most renowned confections only adds to the enjoyment of transforming desserts from their plate form to their full cocktail potential.

Barware

Before creating these cocktails, you should equip yourself with the proper tools and glassware to ensure the best outcome when you mix drinks. This isn't to say that you have to break the bank and outfit your home bar with elaborate items, but having a few staples on hand is a good idea. Below, you will find items that belong in a well-stocked, ready-for-action home bar.

SHAKER

The shaker is by far the most important piece of equipment you will need to create the cocktails in *Liquid Dessert*. I prefer the Boston shaker, which is a two-piece shaker, along with a Hawthorne strainer. Of course, you can use the cobbler shaker with the built-in strainer if you prefer. Also, a julep strainer is nice to have to strain stirred drinks from a mixing glass.

BAR SPOON

A home bar is not complete without at least one long-handled bar spoon. This spoon is extremely handy when it comes to stirring cocktails with ice in a mixing glass. Also, many cocktails call for a *float*, which is when liquid is poured slowly over the back of a bar spoon and into your cocktail.

JIGGER

Measuring your liquid ingredients is crucial when creating a properly mixed cocktail. You could invest in speed pourers and work on your free-pour using a count in your head, or you could just buy a metal hourglass jigger with a 1½-ounce measure on one end and ¾-ounce measure on the other (I would definitely go the jigger route).

STRAINER

I love to use fresh ingredients—especially fresh fruit—in cocktails. Freshness is the difference between a so-so cocktail and a great cocktail. When you start muddling fruit and herbs, there are bound to be small bits left over in the mixing glass that you don't want in the cocktail; this is where a small, cone-shaped, fine mesh strainer—or *double strainer*, as it's called—comes in handy. Simply strain your cocktail through the Hawthorne strainer while holding the second cup strainer over the drink. This should eliminate all the fruit residue that might otherwise float in your drink.

MUDDLER

This may be the cheapest, easiest-to-find piece of equipment for your home bar. The muddler serves as *the presser*—the releaser of all oils, juices, and fragrances that will serve as the base for many of your cocktails.

Liquid Dessert

CHANNEL KNIFE (or vegetable peeler)

To get great-looking garnishes—the fun twists and peels that complete the cocktails—you will need your channel knife. Again, this is an easy tool to find in most stores.

PARING KNIFE

The paring knife is also key for making those fancy garnishes. The lemon twists, spirals, wedges, and really any shape garnish you need can be made by cutting and then trimming the peel off whatever fruit you wish to use. This is a great tool for putting the finishing touch on your cocktails.

HAND JUICER

I always use a handheld juicer that works very well to extract the deliciousness from fruits; simply cut the fruit horizontally and press. Handheld juicers come in a variety of sizes, so choose whatever works best for you. Of course, larger fruits can be cut into smaller pieces to fit your juicer.

GLASSWARE

My wife will tell you what a fan I am of glassware. I love searching for unique pieces that will work for cocktails, but there are definitely a few staple items you should have in your cabinet: martini, coupe, wine, champagne, collins, rocks, and highball glasses. Also, a few of the cocktails in *Liquid Dessert* call for a goblet-style glass.

ICE MOLDS

The ice mold (I have several types at home) allows you to get creative and play around with different forms. I would suggest having at least two standard molds—the round ice mold and the square mold. Not only will the resulting ice make your cocktail look polished and impress your friends, but it will melt more slowly than average ice cubes and won't dilute your drink as quickly.

SYRUP RECIPES FOR THE COCKTAILS

Recipes for the various syrups used in the cocktail recipes may be found in the section titled "Recipes for Syrups" at the end of the book.

channel knife

jigger

jigger with handle

bar spoon

Hawthorne
strainer

peeler

muddler

chapter 1

North America

United States

Bananas Foster

New Orleans is a fascinating city that began as a territory claimed for the French by Robert de La Salle in the 1690s; proprietorship was granted to the Company of the West—the Mississippi Company, as it would come to be known—by the King of France. Jean-Baptiste Le Moyne, also known as Sieur de Bienville, was appointed commandant and director general of the new French colony, and the region was governed by France until 1763, when it was sold to Spain. You will notice when walking around New Orleans that many of the streets are named in honor of Catholic saints and royal houses of France. The most famous street in New Orleans—Bourbon Street—is not actually named for the spirit, but after the Royal House of Bourbon, the family that occupied the throne in France at the time.

The Louisiana Purchase in 1803 marked the arrival of Americans in New Orleans, and their presence was not exactly welcomed, as they were viewed as low class by the Spanish and French Creoles. They disliked the "uncultured" Americans so much that they built Canal Street at the upriver edge of the

French Quarter as a means of keeping the Americans out of the old city. When visiting New Orleans, you will notice the street signs change from *rues* to *streets* as you cross over Canal Street.

Slaves in New Orleans, under less restrictive and more liberal Creole codes, were in some cases allowed to buy their freedom, unlike the slaves under the Americans' rule. There were therefore many free people of color in New Orleans, which made the city unique, especially given its geographical location in the Deep South. This mix of culture and races spawned an incredible collaboration of people with unique talents and inspirations, making the Big Easy one of a kind to this day.

If you're visiting New Orleans, there are a few things you just have to do: visit Café du Monde in the French Market, listen to amazing street jazz, and enjoy dinner at Brennan's Restaurant on Bourbon Street, where you will be treated to a true New Orleans classic—bananas foster. The dessert was invented there in 1951, when Owen Brennan asked his sister to help him create a fancy dessert in honor of the new chairman of the New Orleans Crime Commission, Richard Foster. After scrambling for ideas in the kitchen, Ella Brennan saw a few bananas and recalled a dessert her mother made using split bananas, butter, and brown sugar. For a bit of New Orleans flair, rum and banana liqueur were added to the mix, and the dessert was lit on fire tableside to the enjoyment of customers.

My wife and I drove to New Orleans from Virginia, and we can tell you firsthand that the bananas foster at Brennan's lives up to the hype. I created the bananas foster cocktail using the staples that have made the dessert iconic around the world: fresh bananas, aged rum, cinnamon, and cream. I chose to not include banana liqueur in the cocktail, as I wanted to highlight the deliciousness of the fresh banana puree. What bananas foster cocktail would be complete without being flambéed? Banana slices are soaked in high-proof rum and ignited just prior to serving. As they say in New Orleans, "Pass a good time!"

Bananas Foster: The Cocktail

2 oz aged rum
1½ oz banana puree
1 oz brown sugar simple syrup (see page 135)
1 oz cream
2 dashes of cinnamon
3 slices of banana (garnish)

Directions Combine all ingredients in a mixing glass with ice. Shake well and strain into a coupe glass. For flaming banana garnish, soak banana slices in high-proof rum—I use 100 proof spiced rum—then place on a cocktail spear and rest on the rim of the drink. Light the bananas just as you are ready to serve, then drop bananas in the cocktail to extinguish the flame.

Key Lime Pie

THE FLORIDA KEYS ARE KNOWN for many things: being the site of Hemingway's home, Duval Street, their iconic beaches, and, of course, key lime pie. The first European to come upon Key West was Juan Ponce de León in 1521 during his expedition to Florida while on a mission to find the Fountain of Youth. He named the island Cayo Hueso—Bone Island—on account of the human remains the Europeans found when they came ashore, as the native people did not bury the dead. It later became known as Key West, which sounded like Cayo Hueso to the English-speaking settlers who later took over the Spanish territory.

Due to the shallow reefs just offshore of Old Town and its proximity to the Gulf of Mexico and Atlantic Ocean, Key West became the richest city in the United States per capita during the mid-1800s, thanks to salt manufacturing, wrecking, turtling, and salvaging.

In 1845, construction began on Fort Zachary Taylor, a naval fort at the southern edge of Old Town Key West. The State of Florida joined the Confederacy, though Key West remained a Union territory because of the island's strong naval presence. Key West's link to Cuba was also established during this time, as Cuban refugees of the Ten Years' War took shelter in Old Town Key West. To this day, quite a few historic Cuban-owned businesses and landmarks exist, including San Carlos Institute and Kino Sandals on Duval Street, along with Pepe's, the island's oldest restaurant, which opened in 1909.

Renowned musicians, writers, and dignitaries were attracted to Old Town Key West. Ernest Hemingway and his second wife, Pauline, first visited Key West in 1928. They spent most of the 1930s in a home on Whitehead Street that is still open to the public today. Playwright Tennessee Williams became a regular visitor starting in 1941; this is where he wrote the first draft of *A Streetcar Named Desire*. President Harry S. Truman began making regular visits to Old Town Key West in 1946 during his presidency, eventually transforming the naval station's command headquarters into an official Little White House. Throughout the 1970s and 1980s, Key West came into its own as an offbeat destination for dreamers who wanted to live by their own rules, including Jimmy Buffett, who arrived in 1971.

Many believe the iconic key lime pie dessert owes its roots entirely to Florida, but its true origin is a bit muddled. Evidence suggests that Floridians aren't actually responsible for the inception of the renowned dessert made with key limes, condensed milk, and a graham cracker crust; in fact, key lime pie may have originated from a much more surprising place: a milk company. Stella Parks, author of *BraveTart: Iconic American Desserts*, argues that the Borden milk company invented the recipe to sell more sweetened condensed milk, a crucial ingredient in key lime pie. Naturally, Floridians were not happy with the idea of their trademark dessert originating as a spin-off of the Magic Lemon Cream Pie in a test kitchen in New York City in 1931. The hunt was on to find recipes for key lime pie predating the 1931 recipe, but thus far, the earliest recipe for a key lime pie created in Florida is dated 1933.

No cocktail inspired by the iconic key lime dessert would be complete without using—you guessed it—key limes. I added a bit of fresh orange juice to help balance the lime juice and of course garnished the rim with graham cracker crumbs; the graham cracker crust is a staple of any delicious key lime pie. The coconut cream really helps the cocktail shine and adds a bit of the taste of the tropics we've come to associate with southern Florida.

Key Lime Pie: The Cocktail

2 oz vanilla vodka

1 oz simple syrup (see page 137)

¾ oz fresh key lime juice

½ oz fresh orange juice

½ oz coconut cream (unsweetened)

1 oz heavy cream

graham crackers (crushed for rim)

lime wheel (garnish)

Directions Combine all ingredients in a mixing glass with ice. Shake well and strain into a martini glass rimmed with ground graham crackers (use a cut lime wedge to moisten the rim of the glass before dipping it into ground graham crackers). Garnish with a lime wheel.

Carrot Cake

WHEN CHOOSING A DESSERT to indulge in after a meal, why not choose carrot cake, right? It's the healthy alternative—it has a vegetable right there in the name! So maybe it's not the healthiest of post-entree options, but it is undeniably delicious. Since the modern-day carrot was developed most likely in Persia, or Iran and Afghanistan, some of the oldest recipes hail from the Middle East, but they are very different from the carrot cake we find on our plate today.

During the Middle Ages, roughly AD 500–1500, sugar was scarce in Europe, so carrots were used to sweeten the cakes and puddings. This is where we got the roots of our modern carrot cake recipe. Carrots remained so popular that the British Ministry of Food ran a campaign in the 1940s encouraging people to eat carrots, citing their ability to improve eyesight and enable people to see in the dark; though not 100 percent accurate, it did get lots of people to eat their carrots! When sugar was rationed to eight ounces or 230 grams per week, carrots were commonly used to sweeten cakes and cookies.

In 1783, George Washington, the first president of the United States, indulged in a generous slice of carrot tea cake while dining at the Fraunces Tavern in Lower Manhattan in honor of British Evacuation Day. The recipe came from either an adaptation of a medieval English baked carrot pudding or of the spicy steamed puddings from Europe.

Carrot cake did not enter the American culinary mainstream until the 1960s, when people became familiarized with the importance of proper nutrients in their diets. It seemed rational to assume that a dessert containing carrots was a healthy alternative. Those who assumed it was healthy believed that the carotene in the carrots canceled out the calories in the butter, flour, and sugar. Carrot cake remains a preference by those believing it to be a healthy substitute to other desserts, similar to how Diet Coke is thought to be the healthier alternative to Coke.

Carrot cake is loaded with lots of very different flavors that all come together to create the classic dessert we know and love. My goal with creating the carrot cake cocktail was to deconstruct the dessert and highlight the most prominent flavors. Rum, along with vanilla vodka and carrot juice, pairs nicely with the brown sugar walnut simple syrup, cinnamon, and ginger. No carrot cake is complete without a delicious icing, which is why I chose to include cream in the drink; the resulting concoction is one I think even George Washington would enjoy!

Carrot Cake: The Cocktail

1 oz vanilla vodka
1 oz white rum
1½ oz carrot juice
1 oz cream
¾ brown sugar walnut simple syrup (see page 136)
4 slices of ginger (divided)
3 dashes of cinnamon

Directions In a mixing glass, muddle 2 slices of the ginger. Add remaining ingredients, shake well, and strain into a coupe glass. Garnish with remaining 2 slices of ginger on a cocktail spear.

Peach Cobbler

COBBLERS WERE NEVER MEANT TO be aesthetically appealing. Emerging as a makeshift version of the famous pie recipe cir-cu-lating Europe and the United States in the 1800s, the dessert was *cobbled* together by the early American settlers with fruit— usually canned, preserved, or dried—and clumps of biscuit dough that were baked over an open fire.

In Colonial America, many English settlers did not like the idea of eating raw fruit. During an outbreak of the plague in 1569, for instance, the English made it illegal to sell fresh fruit, and many didn't like the taste of fresh fruit. As a result, people made pies, tarts, jams, and jellies, adding sugar and cooking it by any means necessary. The cobbler is said to have been an im-provisation of the much-loved pie into a trail-modified dessert. Fruit, in whatever form, was tossed into a Dutch oven, topped with globs of biscuit dough, and baked over an open fire until golden brown. Cobblers were quickly integrated into the settler diet, with many choosing to eat the sweet dish for all meals of the day. The cobbler was a good way for the English settlers to cope with conditions on the American frontier, and it wasn't until the late nineteenth century that the cobbler was officially labeled as a dessert.

Some homes had a kitchen hearth with a beehive oven built into the fireplace wall, and others had an outdoor brick oven. However, many homes, even among those wealthy enough to own slaves, had no oven at all; all baking was done in iron pots over the hot coals in the open hearth. Sliced peaches would be placed at the bottom of the pot, and then biscuit dough—

perhaps left over from breakfast—would be dropped over the fruit.

By the 1950s, peach cobbler had become an American dessert staple, and in an effort to sell more canned peaches, the Georgia Peach Council declared April 13 National Peach Cobbler Day. Today, peach cobbler is a traditional dessert served in the Deep South, usually accompanied by a scoop of vanilla ice cream.

When I hear *peach cobbler*, I immediately think of the American South, and there is no spirit more popular in the South than bourbon whiskey. Kentucky alone produces 95 percent of the world's bourbon, so it was only fitting to highlight the Southern staple in the cocktail devoted to peach cobbler. My goal was to cobble together a delicious drink by adding brown sugar and lemon juice to complement the bourbon and peach. The drink uses crushed ice in the traditional cobbler fashion and relies heavily on the ripeness of the peach.

Peach Cobbler: The Cocktail

2 oz bourbon
¼ peach (muddled)
¼ oz brown sugar simple syrup (see page 135)
¼ oz lemon juice
2 dashes of cinnamon
mint sprig (garnish)
peach slice (garnish)

Directions Muddle the peach in a mixing glass with ice. Add remaining ingredients, shake well, and strain over crushed ice in a rocks glass. Garnish with peach and mint sprig.

Pumpkin Pie

IT'S HARD TO IMAGINE AN American Thanksgiving table without the pervasive rich orange custard made from strained, spiced, and twice-cooked squash. Ah, pumpkin pie—an American staple. Few of our foods can claim deeper American roots than pumpkins, which were first cultivated in Central America around 5500 BC and were one of the earliest foods European explorers brought back from the New World. The orange gourds were first mentioned in Europe around 1536, and within a few decades, they were grown regularly in England.

When the Pilgrims sailed for America on the Mayflower in 1620, it's likely some of them were as familiar with pumpkins as the Wampanoag, who helped them survive their first year at Plymouth Colony. A year later, when the fifty surviving colonists were joined by a group of ninety Wampanoag for a three-day harvest celebration, it is likely that pumpkin was on the table in one form or another.

By the seventeenth century, pumpkin pie was already appearing in cookbooks. Over the course of the next two centuries, pumpkin pie's fame grew with the rising popularity of Thanksgiving. It wasn't until the release of Amelia Simmons's cookbook in 1796, *American Cookery*—the first cookbook by an American to be published in the United States—that the pie became nationally recognized as an American Thanksgiving hallmark. Simmons's book contained two recipes for pumpkin pie, one of which closely resembles the recipes we use today.

Legend has it that in the early eighteenth century, a small town in Connecticut postponed its Thanksgiving for a week because there wasn't enough molasses available to make pumpkin pie. Many women's magazines began featuring recipes for pumpkin pie, and Libby's meat-canning company developed the first line of canned pumpkin, releasing it in 1929.

No cocktail inspired by pumpkin pie would be complete without pumpkin puree and aged rum. I chose Jamaican rum as the base spirit, since the Pilgrims captured the island of Santiago, now known as Jamaica, for the British Empire, solidifying rum as a spirit of choice for colonists for hundreds of years thereafter. Because pumpkin pie is a custard, I included heavy cream to give the cocktail a thicker texture. A pumpkin pie cocktail needs a little spice, so I added cinnamon and Angostura bitters.

Pumpkin Pie: The Cocktail

2 oz Jamaican aged rum
1½ oz brown sugar simple syrup (see page 135)
1½ oz pumpkin puree
¾ oz heavy cream
3 thin slices of ginger
3 dashes of cinnamon
1 dash of Angostura bitters
3 whole cranberries (garnish)

Directions Muddle the ginger in a mixing glass.
Add remaining ingredients with ice and shake well.
Strain into a coupe glass and garnish with 3 whole
cranberries on a cocktail spear.

Liquid Dessert

Mexico

Churros

Mexican dessert enjoyed at street carts and high-end restaurants alike. Traditional churros can be thick or thin and are deep-fried. They are then sprinkled with sugar and served alone or with drinks like café con leche, hot chocolate, or champurrado, a thick chocolate-based drink.

History is divided on exactly how churros came to exist. Some say they were the invention of nomadic Spanish shepherds. Living high in the mountains with no access to bakeries, the Spanish shepherds supposedly created churros, which were simple for them to cook in frying pans over fire. This version of history is deemed credible because there exists a breed of sheep called the Navajo-Churro that are descended from the Churra sheep of the Iberian Peninsula; the horns of these sheep look like the fried pastry.

Another legend says that Portuguese sailors discovered a similar food in Northern China called You Tiao, which they brought back with them. The Spanish learned of the new culinary treat from their neighbors and put their own spin on it by passing the dough through a star-shaped tip, which gives the churro its signature ridges.

Churros were introduced to Mexico by Spanish explorers like Hernán Cortés around the 1500s during the Spanish Inquisition. The confections were embraced by Aztecs, Mayans, and other local tribes. In Mexico, explorers discovered cacao, which they took back to Europe and used to make the hot chocolate and chocolate sauces sometimes served with churros.

The modern-day churro has undergone various iterations, including a guava-filled version in Cuba, one that is cheese-stuffed in Uruguay, and dulce de leche–filled confections in Mexico.

When creating the cocktail, I aimed to highlight what makes the churro special—that delicious cinnamon flavor. I married tequila with a very small amount of Goldschläger to get that cinnamon flavor while paying homage to Mexico's most brilliant creation: tequila. The cream and brown sugar help mellow the strong flavors, while the Godiva contributes a nice sweetness. Add a finishing touch to the cocktail by dipping the rim of a coupe glass in the cream and lining the rim with cinnamon sugar prior to shaking the drink.

Churros: The Cocktail

1½ oz blanco tequila

1 oz Godiva Chocolate Liqueur

¼ oz Goldschläger

1 oz heavy cream

¾ oz brown sugar simple syrup (see page 135)

cinnamon sugar (for rim)

Directions Rim a coupe glass with cinnamon sugar. Add all ingredients in a mixing glass. Shake well and strain into a coupe glass.

Liquid Dessert

Pastel de Tres Leches

PASTEL TRES LECHES CAKE (literally "three milks cake") is a traditional Latin American dessert that you will find in nearly every Mexican bakery, restaurant, and taqueria out there. This rich milk-soaked sponge cake delicacy is served at traditional Mexican weddings and quinceañeras on either side of the border. An authentic tres leches cake recipe will yield a light sponge layer that is perforated after baking and then steeped in three milks: evaporated milk, condensed milk, and heavy cream or whole milk. The cake acts as a giant sponge that soaks up the delicious milk syrup, creating the rich and moist density that gives it an amazing taste. It has often been compared to the Italian dessert of tiramisu, but tres leches cake is most certainly a dessert unique to Latin America.

The original recipe is reported to come from the back of an evaporated or condensed milk can in Latin America to promote the use of the product. Both types of milk were sold throughout Central and South America and the Caribbean. A side note on condensed milk: the product first came into use in the mid-1850s as a way to preserve milk in cans without refrigeration. Evaporated milk became available during the 1870s, when milk companies were able to heat it so that it would not spoil in the cans, thereby making the sugar unnecessary. They both became an immediate success in urban areas, where fresh milk was difficult to distribute and store.

Those who grew up in Mexico and the bordering states will tell you that *pastel de tres leches* was the cake they could expect

to be served at any major events, such as birthdays, graduations, and weddings, and the cake has become the centerpiece of any celebration, family gathering, or fiesta.

If you see a *pastel de tres leches* nearby, you know you are at a special event. The decadent sponge cake that is soaked in three different types of milk is a staple at any major festivity in Mexico and other countries around the world. Unsurprisingly, the cocktail I made for the dessert uses—you guessed it—three different types of milk. If you are not familiar with RumChata, it is a delicious blend of Wisconsin dairy cream, Mexican spices, and Caribbean rum, and it is perfect to mix with a light rum, heavy cream, and sweetened condensed milk. Enjoy the festivities, whatever they may be!

Pastel de Tres Leches: The Cocktail

1½ oz RumChata
½ oz white rum
¾ oz sweetened condensed milk
1½ oz heavy cream
strawberries (garnish)
kiwis (garnish)

Directions Combine all ingredients in a mixing glass with ice. Shake well and strain into a goblet. Garnish with strawberries and kiwis on a cocktail spear.

Caramel Flan

FLAN IS THE MOST POPULAR Latin dessert and has been for many generations; for anyone wondering, flan is traditionally pronounced in a way that rhymes with *lawn*. The dessert is made everywhere, from the old ranches of rural Mexico to the upscale restaurants of major cities in South America and all around the world.

Flan was created during the Roman Empire, as the Romans were the first to domesticate chickens; thus, they found themselves in the middle of an egg surplus. Using techniques stolen from the Greeks, the Romans developed new egg-based recipes. These recipes resulted in many different dishes and desserts, flan included.

Around this time, most versions of the dessert were savory rather than sweet and included flavors like eel sprinkled with pepper—delicious! There are a few early recorded recipes containing honey, the only sweetener of the day. As the Romans continued their conquest of much of Europe, their beliefs, customs, and recipes traveled with them. This novel sweet variety of flan impressed those in the newly vanquished lands, and when the Empire fell in AD 476, flan managed to survive.

The Spanish were particularly taken with flan and were the first to top it with a caramel sauce. Like the Romans before them, the Spaniards brought flan to new lands. In 1518, conquistador Hernán Cortés landed in the Yucatan Peninsula of Mexico. Soon after, Mexican cooks took the dessert to a whole new level, and the Mexican flan became a highly improved version of the Roman and Spanish forms of the dessert. Mexican cooks created coffee, chocolate, and coconut flavors, and the recipes became popular not only in Mexico but also in the rest of Latin America.

A cocktail devoted to caramel flan must have a thick texture similar to that of the custard we find on our table when we order flan in a restaurant or make it at home. Heavy cream and a whole egg both help achieve this texture in the cocktail. It is very important to dry shake (using no ice) to emulsify the egg prior to adding the ice and other ingredients. I found that apricot brandy brought a light fruit flavor to balance out the rum and caramel flavors. Finish off the cocktail with a light drizzle of the caramel sauce and enjoy this liquid version of a classic.

Caramel Flan: The Cocktail

2 oz aged rum
1½ oz caramel sauce*
1½ oz heavy cream
¼ oz apricot brandy
1 whole egg
caramel sauce drizzle (on top of drink)

Directions Add the whole egg to a mixing glass
and vigorously dry shake (no ice) for 20 seconds.
Add ice and remaining ingredients and shake well.
Strain into a coupe glass and drizzle the caramel
sauce on top of the cocktail.

*Caramel sauce In a saucepan over medium heat,
combine 1 cup packed brown sugar, ½ cup milk,
4 tablespoons unsalted butter, 1 teaspoon vanilla,
and a pinch of salt. Stir constantly until dissolved,
then simmer over medium-low heat for 10 minutes,
stirring gently. Let cool prior to using.

Canada

Québec Sugar Pie

QUÉBEC SUGAR PIE IS A Canadian classic. Also known as tarte au sucre, the pie features a flaky, buttery crust. The pie filling is typically made of eggs, cream, sugar, butter, flour, and vanilla—all the delicious basics! Like most Québecois cuisine, sugar pie is an adaptation of recipes from northwest France, where most of Québec's settlers originated. In 1789, the British conquered the French in Québec, and the resultant food culture would marry the two countries' influences with indigenous staples like corn and squash.

The province of Québec has an old-world sensibility flowing through it that sets it apart from the rest of Canada. Québecois food—like the classic poutine, which is North American French fries covered in a brown gravy and topped with cheese curds—perfectly illustrates the area's mix of influences.

For many early Canadians, maple was the only form of sugar, and it was used in every dessert, the most basic of which was maple syrup drizzled on fresh snow and rolled into candy. Canada produces about 80 percent of the world's pure maple syrup, and Québec alone is responsible for over 90 percent of the country's production. Canadians enjoy "sugar shacking"—*cabane au sucre*—in the springtime to enjoy the abundant syrup provided by the maple trees.

The traditional French Canadian diet is rich in calories with a high sugar and fat content, which was necessary for the early Québec settlers to survive the harsh elements. The high sugar also served as a counterbalance to the brutal conditions of life—a taste of sweetness for the joie de vivre.

What distinguishes the French Canadian version of many desserts is the use of maple sugar or syrup as the sweetening agent. Brown sugar was hard to find in the early days in Canada and was unavailable in Québec. Over time, brown sugar has gradually come to replace the maple flavor, so tarte au sucre—originally made with maple syrup—now contains brown sugar.

Canada is known for many things, but maybe no two items are more associated with Canada than hockey and maple syrup. Should you have the opportunity to eat a slice of Québec sugar pie while watching a hockey game—well that's grounds for citizenship! I really enjoy Canadian whisky, as the laws governing what makes a whiskey Canadian are somewhat lax, so each bottle you try can vary wildly, which keeps things interesting. For the cocktail, I added a bit of fresh lemon juice and egg white to complement the sweetness of the maple syrup and brown sugar.

Québec Sugar Pie: The Cocktail

2½ oz Canadian whisky
¾ oz brown sugar
¾ oz pure maple syrup
1 oz cream
¼ oz fresh lemon juice
1 egg white
lemon twist (garnish)

Directions Dry shake (no ice) the egg white. Add remaining ingredients with ice. Shake well and strain into martini glass. Garnish with lemon twist.

Nanaimo Bar

THE CANADIAN CITY OF Nanaimo, in British Columbia, was an outpost of the Hudson's Bay Company and was a coal-mining center and timber town. However, Nanaimo's place in history may be forever entwined with its culinary namesake. A traditional Nanaimo bar consists of a layer of coconut, a layer of soft yellow custard in the middle, a graham crust on the bottom, and a layer of chocolate ganache on top.

Across Canada, you will find the sugary bars for sale everywhere, from small-town gas stations, to school bake sales, to Starbucks and supermarkets, where they compete with Nanaimo bar baking kits. In 2017, the Tim Hortons restaurant chain created a doughnut filled with the flavors of the Nanaimo bar for the nation's 150th anniversary. In 2006, it was voted Canada's favorite dessert in a *National Post* poll, and one journalist called the bars "the hockey of desserts."

The Nanaimo bar has been tagged a New York slice, a London fog bar, a chocolate square, and a prayer bar, but the city of Nanaimo has been instrumental in ensuring this delicious dessert option is named the Nanaimo bar and sealing its place in Canadian food history. Visitors and locals alike can take a self-guided tour through the streets of Nanaimo, as the Nanaimo Bar Trail lets participants taste the many creative interpretations of the famous treat along thirty-nine different stops.

As part of Canada Post's Sweet Canada stamp collection, Nanaimo's legendary bar even has its own stamp. The collection features a total of ten famous Canadian desserts, and the stamp itself features a variation of a Nanaimo bar, rather than a traditional bar, which stirred up a bit of controversy.

I spent my freshman year of college in British Columbia attending the University of Victoria on Vancouver Island, so I can attest to the popularity of the Nanaimo bar in Canada. It is truly a staple. With layers of chocolate ganache, sweet custard, coconut, and graham, the dessert is fantastic and translates naturally to the glass. The bottom of the glass holds a little extra chocolate for all the chocolate lovers out there and contributes to the layered look of the cocktail.

Nanaimo Bar: The Cocktail

2 oz vodka

1 oz cream of coconut

1 oz Godiva dark chocolate liqueur

1 oz heavy cream

¾ oz dulce de leche (see page 136)

¼ oz amaretto

Lyons chocolate dessert sauce

chocolate graham crackers (crushed for rim)

Directions Prior to mixing the drink, dip martini glass in milk to coat the rim and garnish with crushed chocolate graham crackers. Using chocolate sauce, fill bottom ½ inch of martini glass. Add all ingredients to a shaker with ice. Shake well and strain into martini glass.

Blueberry Grunt

A BLUEBERRY GRUNT IS A Canadian blueberry cobbler. What sets it apart from a blueberry cobbler is that the dumplings steam rather than bake. The simmering blueberries make a grunt-like sound while boiling under the dumplings as the steam moves through the dumpling batter. In other words, a grunt is just another name for a cobbler, but all grunts are made on the stovetop, whereas cobblers are typically baked. A grunt can also be called a slump, depending on where in the Maritimes you live.

Canada is the world's largest producer of wild lowbush blueberries. Most are grown commercially in Québec and the Atlantic provinces. They are native to Eastern North America and grow best on treeless or burned-over land.

The origins of the blueberry grunt are unclear. Many claim that it was first made by early colonial settlers as an adaptation of British pudding using local ingredients; others claim it originated as a form of Acadian forage food. The truth likely lies somewhere in the middle. The blueberry grunt became widely popular in Eastern Canada and is still a huge hit today. Of course, there are variations on this classic dish, with the biggest difference being in the volume of ingredients used.

I've always loved peach cobbler and blueberry pie, so it's only natural that I would be a huge fan of the blueberry grunt dessert. I was unaware that the Maritime provinces of Canada—New Brunswick, Nova Scotia, and Prince Edward Island—were brimming with lowbush blueberries. My father is from Montreal, Québec, so although I've heard of the Maritime provinces, we never actually spent time in this region. I enjoy a blueberry pie

with fresh lemon zest, which is why I used limoncello and fresh lemon juice in the cocktail. The thyme gives the drink a delicious herbal twist that pairs well with the blueberry simple syrup and vanilla vodka. If you're a fan of blueberries and fresh citrus, you will love mixing up this cocktail!

Blueberry Grunt: The Cocktail

2 oz vanilla vodka

1 oz blueberry simple syrup (see page 135)

¾ oz fresh lemon juice

¼ oz limoncello

4 thyme sprigs (divided)

2 dashes of cinnamon

lemon twist (garnish)

Directions Add 3 thyme sprigs in a mixing glass with ice. Add remaining ingredients and shake well. Strain over one large ice cube in a rocks glass. Garnish with remaining thyme sprig and lemon twist.

chapter 2

Colombia

Plátanos Calados

Every nation in South America has a distinct culinary tradition shaped by local crops and migrating citizens, but there is one element that unites them all: a serious love for dessert. This makes sense as South America is where cane sugar comes from. Brazil is the world's leading producer of sugarcane, and Colombia, Ecuador, Venezuela, and Peru have a long history of growing the plant along the Pacific and Caribbean coastlines.

Plátanos calados, or plantains with brown sugar syrup, showcase the rich flavor of the sweet plantain. Extremely ripe—nearly black—plantains are combined with brown or muscovado sugar, clove, water, cinnamon, and lemon juice, then simmered until a syrup forms. This process results in a soft and sweet banana that highlights the spicy flavors of the clove and cinnamon. The dish is served as is or with a soft white cheese. Most Latin American countries offer some version of caramelized sweet plantains. Bananas, plantains, and banana leaves are deeply ingrained in Latin American cuisine. As a side note, plantains are denser than bananas and are mostly used in cooking; bananas are typically eaten as fruit.

Bananas and plantains have become staples across the tropical climates of the Caribbean and Central America, likely due to their versatility, starchy texture, and high nutritional value. Bananas and plantains were a cheap source of food for the slave population of the Caribbean, and they are used in Caribbean cuisine to this day.

Plantains and bananas are very versatile. I was excited to introduce brandy to the mix when creating the plátanos calados cocktail, along with aged rum and brown sugar simple syrup; the brown sugar is a staple in the dessert. The fresh lemon juice helps balance the sweetness. This cocktail will not disappoint. Cheers!

Plátanos Calados: The Cocktail

1 oz brandy

1 oz aged rum

1 oz plantain puree

1 oz brown sugar simple syrup (see page 135)

½ oz lemon juice

3 dashes of cinnamon

cinnamon stick (garnish)

lemon twist (garnish)

Directions Shake all ingredients in a mixing glass with ice. Using a fine mesh sieve to get rid of plantain bits, strain into a coupe glass. Garnish with lemon twist and cinnamon stick.

Liquid Dessert

Uruguay

Chajá

CHAJÁ IS A URUGUAYAN DESSERT that consists of three layers of sponge cake stuffed with syrup, peaches, dulce de leche, and whipped cream, then topped with peaches. The cake is a staple at Uruguayan feasts and celebrations. Chaja was invented by Orlando Castellano in the late 1920s. Castellano was the owner of the pastry shop Las Familias in Paysandú, one of the main cities in Uruguay.

The name of this cake was inspired by an aboriginal term for a typical bird of the region. The bird—the *chajá*, or southern screamer—could easily be the symbol of the Southern Cone, the southernmost zone of the South American continent. The chajá bird is large with thick plumage. Although it appears formidable, it is very light due to its hollow bones; it weighs only eight pounds as an adult. Castellano named his cake after the odd-looking bird, which has pockets of air under its skin, because it reminded him of the light and airy meringue in the cake.

Cachaça, or fermented sugarcane juice that has been distilled, is hugely popular in South America. It is unfortunate that we rarely see this spirit on cocktail menus in the United

States, unless of course we're talking about the caipirinha, the national cocktail of Brazil. The spirit is highly unique and becomes more delightful with each sip. I was excited to pair cachaça with peaches and cream and am very happy with the result. The homemade meringue looks great as a garnish, gives the cocktail a nice airy quality, and can be eaten on the side with the peaches.

Chajá: The Cocktail

1 oz cachaça
1 oz peach syrup (from can)
¾ oz dulce de leche (see page 136)
¾ oz heavy cream
2 peach slices (from can, muddled)
meringue* (homemade, garnish)

Directions Muddle the peaches in a mixing glass. Add remaining ingredients, shake well, and strain into large coupe glass. Garnish with dollops of homemade meringue and 3 peach slices to cover half of the rim.

*Meringue Beat 3 egg whites in a medium bowl with an electric mixer until frothy. Add ¼ teaspoon cream of tartar and beat until soft peaks form. Gradually beat in ¼ cup sugar, 1 tablespoon at a time. Continue to beat until sugar is dissolved and stiff peaks form. Refrigerate until ready to use.

Peru

Picarones

PICARONES ARE SIMILAR TO doughnuts in shape and texture, and the treats are a favorite dessert of Peruvians; in fact, the dessert is considered one of the most traditional and exquisite of Peruvian pastries. Bathed in chancaca (unrefined sugar) and honey, this delicacy made from pumpkin and sweet potato has always held a top spot in the popular culture of this country.

Legend has it that the picarón has its origin in pre-Hispanic times, when the ancient natives prepared a similar recipe with squash and sweet potatoes, which were part of the Incan diet. Later, with the arrival of the Spaniards, new ingredients such as wheat flour and sugar were added. During the nearly three hundred years that Peru spent under Spanish rule, Spaniards introduced deep-fried dough balls called buñuelos to the region. As they colonized the nation, the Spaniards brought African slaves, and it was the enslaved African cooks who reworked the original buñuelos recipe to incorporate Peruvian sweet potato and squash. They kneaded flour and salt with mashed produce and fried spoonfuls of the orange dough in hot lard, then finished off the delicious treat by dousing the crisp exterior in sweet syrup.

Peru regained independence from Spain in the nineteenth century, and the modified buñuelos, now known as picarones, had become an integral part of Afro-Peruvian culture. Families passed down recipes through generations, and picarones made their way into harvest festivals and religious processions and throughout the streets. Today, picarones are in such hot demand by Peruvians and foreigners that you will find the confection at street stalls in every corner of Lima, the capital, where they prepare it in a few seconds and serve it hot.

I would wager that most cocktail enthusiasts have heard of the pisco sour. Pisco, essentially an unaged brandy, is the national spirit of Peru and is hugely popular across South America. The spirit was created by Spanish settlers who brought their own grapevines to South America and distilled the leftover grapes that could not be used for wine. Of course, pisco had to be incorporated into the cocktail honoring picarones, as did a sweet potato simple syrup, which may sound involved but is actually very simple to make.

Picarones: The Cocktail

¾ oz pisco
¾ oz aged rum
¾ oz sweet potato simple syrup (see page 137)
¾ oz canned pumpkin puree
½ oz fresh lime juice
1 dash of allspice
lime wheel (garnish)

Directions Add all ingredients in a mixing glass with ice. Shake well and strain over 3 or 4 large cubes in a round rocks glass. Garnish with lime wheel.

Suspiro de Limeña

SUSPIRO DE LIMEÑA IS a Peruvian dessert that originated in the city of Lima and is based on *manjar blanco*, the Peruvian name for what is known as dulce de leche in other parts of South America. Creamy, caramel-like pudding, or dulce de leche, is topped with a port-flavored meringue and sprinkled with a touch of cinnamon. Meringue plays a big part in suspiro de limeña, which was also brought to Peru by the Spaniards. Renowned for its intense flavors, this delicacy can be found in all restaurants in Lima and is often paired with a cup of iced tea or a glass of pisco. The recipe's slow cooking process results in a golden, silky smooth custard base, which is then crowned with a light and creamy liqueur meringue.

The origin of suspiro de limeña (meaning "sigh of Lima") dates back to the beginning of the nineteenth century, although most of its ingredients were brought from Spain during the colonial period. The word *limeña*, pronounced lee-main-ya, also means a female resident of Lima, Peru. The dessert's name comes from the Peruvian writer and poet José Gálvez Barrenechea. When he tried the dessert—which was prepared by his wife, Amparo Ayarez, an expert cook who devised the recipe—for the first time, he was so delighted with the flavors that he described its texture with a romantic verse: "A soft and sweet sigh of a woman." However, the first known record of the recipe appeared in the *New Dictionary of American Cuisine*, published in 1818, where this dessert was named *manjar real del Peru* (royal delight of Peru).

I think port wines are widely underused in cocktails today. The fortified wines are varied and complex and can provide a delicious nutty flavor, as is the case with the tawny port I use for the cocktail devoted to the Peruvian suspiro de limeña dessert. I really like the combination of port and pisco (of course pisco had to make its presence known in another dessert staple of Peru). The egg white, when dry shaken prior to adding ice, adds a nice texture to the drink.

Suspiro de Limeña: The Cocktail

1½ oz tawny port wine
½ oz pisco
1 oz dulce de leche (see page 136)
1½ oz heavy cream
1 egg white
2 dashes of cinnamon
cinnamon (dusting as garnish)

Directions Dry shake (no ice) all ingredients for 15 seconds. Add ice and shake well. Strain into a coupe glass and garnish with a dusting of cinnamon.

Argentina

Chocotorta

A NO-BAKE ARGENTINIAN dessert, chocotorta (chocolate cake), was influenced by Italian cuisine and modeled on the famous Italian tiramisu. It is made with three staple Argentinian ingredients: chocolate biscuits, dulce de leche, and cream cheese. A regular at most Argentinian celebrations and birthday parties, it is famous in Argentina but hard to find, as it's something most people cook at home but few restaurants offer.

Marité Mabragaña, who was an advertising executive with the ad agency Ricardo de Luca, created a commercial in 1982 introducing the Argentinian dessert called chocotorta. Mabragaña is also credited with being the first in Argentina to successfully co-brand products; it was her idea to combine two of her accounts—Mendizábal, the makers of Mendicrim cream cheese, and Bagley, the makers of Chocolinas chocolate cookies—in one commercial. Using her knowledge of Italian desserts, particularly tiramisu, she developed a no-cook cake, and the chocotorta was born.

The chocotorta is assembled with Chocolinas, which are rectangular chocolate biscuits that are commonly dipped in coffee or tea and enjoyed as a traditional Argentinian dessert. Although chocotorta is popular in the country and translates as *choco-late cake*, the dessert is not without controversy. The debate is whether or not this dessert deserves the right to be referred to as a cake or belongs to a no-bake dessert category.

If you are a fan of everything chocolate, you are going to love the cocktail for chocotorta. I included espresso vodka to pay homage to tiramisu, the dessert that inspired chocotorta. The Godiva liqueur and rich dulce de leche are combined with the cream and espresso vodka to create a velvety smooth drink to satisfy even the largest chocolate craving.

Chocotorta: The Cocktail

1½ oz espresso vodka
1½ oz Godiva dark chocolate liqueur
1 oz dulce de leche (see page 136)
1 oz heavy cream
chocolate wafer cookies (ground, rim garnish)
Lyons chocolate syrup (garnish)

Directions Prior to mixing the drink, moisten the rim of the martini glass in cream, then dip in the ground wafers to coat the rim. Add chocolate syrup in horizontal lines in a chilled martini glass to resemble the layers of the chocotorta dessert. Combine all ingredients in a mixing glass with ice. Shake well and strain into the martini glass.

chapter 3

Europe

Greece

Revani

R evani is a classic Greek and Turkish dessert made from sugar, semolina, flour, and—depending on recipe variations—additional flavorings such as vanilla, lemon zest, or rose water. The cake is characterized by its overpowering sweetness, the result of being soaked in sugar syrup after it has been baked. Its popularity is widespread among many Jewish and Muslim communities around the world, and Muslims have made it a staple during the holy month of Ramadan.

The most likely origin of the Greek revani can be traced back to the rabani of Turkish cuisine, one of the most classic cakes during the time of the Ottoman Empire. While the entire country enjoys the dessert, the city of Veria is the revani-making capital of Greece.

Revani was first baked by Ottoman pastry chefs to celebrate the conquest of Armenia in the sixteenth century. The name given to this famous dessert comes from the Battle of Revan, the country's capital, now known as Yerevan. Over the years, the cake began to grace many tables during the Ottoman period, and its name was changed from *rabani* to *revani* (the precious).

Ancient Greece has given us many astonishing tools and traditions that we still use today—take geometry, literature, theater, architecture, and democracy, just to name a few—and it's fair to add gastronomy to the list, as the people of Greece know how to cook and create delicious pastries! Revani is a tasty semolina cake based in the Mediterranean and Middle Eastern region. The cake is sweet and airy and is highlighted with flavors of orange and coconut, which you will find in the cocktail below. It is important to use freshly squeezed orange juice, as there is no solid substitute.

Revani: The Cocktail

1 oz vanilla vodka
¾ oz amaretto
¾ oz freshly squeezed orange juice
¾ oz cream of coconut
½ oz lemon juice
1 egg white
orange twist (garnish)

Directions Add all ingredients in a mixing glass.
Dry shake (no ice) for 15 seconds. Add ice and
shake well. Strain into a coupe glass and garnish
with orange twist.

Kataifi

KATAIFI IS A POPULAR Middle Eastern pastry made with a special form of shredded phyllo dough that is also called kataifi. The dessert is similar to baklava in flavor and features nuts mixed with sugar and spices like cinnamon. Kataifi is made from water and wheat flour. This stringy dough comes in the form of long, semicooked vermicelli and is used in many desserts and savory pastries. Most forms of kataifi are sweet; however, some cooks also use the dough to make unique savory appetizers with ground meat or vegetables. After it is cooked, the kataifi is generously soaked in a cinnamon-flavored sugar syrup.

If you order kataifi in Turkey, you will be amazed by how many different ways it can be prepared. In Greece, however, the version is usually rolled up into small pockets. The predecessor of the kataifi we know today has been mentioned in *One Thousand and One Nights*. That version is quite similar to the English crumpet and may even be its ancestor. This pudding-like version of the dessert stuffed with nuts can still be found in Turkey, though under different names, including *yassı kadayıf*, *taş kadayıf*, and *taş ekmeği*.

Kataifi is similar to baklava in flavor, but the main difference lies in the form of the phyllo dough. Tsipouro is an unaged brandy made in Greece; it has a strong anise flavor, so a little goes a long way in terms of using it as a mixing agent in cocktails. The star of this cocktail is the homemade kataifi simple syrup, which infuses nuts, citrus, and spices to balance out the spirits and deliver the delicious flavors that have become synonymous with this famous Middle Eastern dessert.

Kataifi: The Cocktail

1¼ oz brandy

¾ oz tsipouro

1 oz kataifi simple syrup (see page 137)

½ oz lemon juice

Directions Add all ingredients in a mixing glass with ice.
Shake well and strain into a coupe glass.

Turkey

Baklava

THE ORIGIN OF BAKLAVA is a bit hazy, to say the least. A few nations have claimed baklava as their own, including some nations as far as central Asia. That being said, it is generally accepted that the first form of baklava came around 800 BC from the Assyrian Empire, where layers of bread dough were stretched thinly and baked with chopped nuts and honey for special occasions.

The ancient Greeks developed a fondness for the Assyrian delicacy, and it is believed they were the ones who developed an incredibly thin dough called phyllo (meaning "leaf" in Greek), which made the layers lighter and more delicate. The spice and silk routes started to influence the ingredients, with cardamom, rose water, and cinnamon becoming staples of the dessert.

Baklava in some form is made in many countries today, but Turkey is renowned for producing the delicacy. Large sheets of pastry are stretched so thin they become transparent before being buttered and layered on top of one another. Pistachios from Gaziantep, a city in Turkey, Aegean almonds, and hazelnuts or walnuts from the Black Sea Region are used as filling.

Gaziantep, Turkey, is the spiritual home of baklava, especially those made with pistachios, which are world famous and grown in the city. Gaziantep baklavasi was awarded Protected Geographical Indication status by the European Union in 2013. Large teams of bakers roll out the sheets, layer them with the region's pistachios, cut them into diamonds, pour melted butter over them, and place them in the oven before dousing them with syrup and letting them cool.

The Turks absorbed baklava into their culture, and as the Ottoman Turkish Empire expanded far beyond Anatolia, the dessert became a household treat across the Mediterranean and into the Middle East. The Turks treated baklava as a dessert of the wealthy, which makes sense because of the skill needed in making phyllo dough, and the sultan would give it as a special gift. Some bakers even have to apprentice before they are considered ready to make the paper-thin dough by hand. Today, it is more of an everyday dessert for the Turks, while Greeks still reserve baklava for special occasions.

My neighbor, Cecily, a fantastic cook, often brings baklava over to our house around Christmas as a special treat. On one occasion, she invited my mother and wife over to prepare the dessert as a team. It was then that my family learned just how much time and attention go into making the delicacy. Cecily did divulge her secret weapon: a hint of lime to balance the sweetness. I made sure to include her secret in the cocktail devoted to baklava, along with rose water and ground pistachios for the rim of the glass. *Şerefe*!

Baklava: The Cocktail

1½ oz vanilla vodka
½ oz tsipouro
1¼ oz baklava simple syrup (see page 135)
¼ oz honey syrup (see page 136)
¼ oz fresh lime juice
2 dashes of rose water
ground pistachios (garnish)
lime twist (garnish)

Directions Prior to mixing the cocktail, moisten the rim of a martini glass with lime and line the rim with ground pistachios. Combine all ingredients in a shaker with ice. Shake well, then strain into coupe glass. Garnish with ground pistachios on the rim and a lime twist.

Italy

Cannoli

NAPLES IS FAMOUS for its pizza, Rome has *cacio e pepe* (a cheese-and-pepper dish), and Sicily has cannoli. Arguably Italy's most famous dessert, cannoli are proudly put on display in nearly every Sicilian café. Cannoli are deep-fried cylindrical pastry shells filled with sweetened whipped ricotta mixed with chocolate chips, pistachios, and often candied citron. In Sicily, they traditionally used goat's or sheep's milk ricotta, which is considered the most delicious for cannoli, although the fillings vary around the world from cow's milk ricotta to whipped cream, pastry cream, custard, or mascarpone.

In Italian, the word *cannoli* is plural and *cannolo* is singular, but in English they are almost always referred to as *cannoli*. The name comes from *canna*, the river reeds that were cut into sections and used as a mold to fry the pastry shells. Today, commercially available metal tubes are used in place of river reeds.

According to Sicilian tradition, whenever you offer cannoli to guests, there must be at least twelve on the serving plate. Another tradition suggests serving them on a platter piled high in the shape of a Turk's turban—*la testa del turcu* (Turk's head). Sicilians believe more is the best when it comes to cannoli.

As with so many other Sicilian dishes, the dessert's roots can be traced to Saracen times. The Arabs ruled Sicily for most of the tenth and eleventh centuries and introduced sugar and many almond-based sweets to the island. Popular legend states that in the Sicilian city of Caltanissetta during Arab rule (around AD 1000), a harem of women created the dessert comprised of a fried tubular pastry shell made of flour, sugar, and butter and filled with sweet and creamy ricotta cheese to praise their emir's masculinity.

Cannoli spread from Palermo and Messina throughout Sicily and then all of Italy. The dessert came to the United States with the great Sicilian migration in the 1880s and inspired one of the most memorable Hollywood film quotes of all time from *The Godfather*: "Leave the gun. Take the cannoli."

Cannoli are some of the most recognizable desserts on the planet. Even if you haven't seen *The Godfather*, odds are you're familiar with this Italian staple. For the cannoli cocktail, I chose to incorporate a bit of goat's milk, as it is traditionally used in Sicilian cannoli. No cannoli would be complete without a few chocolate chips and delicious homemade whipped cream, which is actually very easy to make. So, in honor of *The Godfather*, put down the beer and pick up the cannoli cocktail.

Cannoli: The Cocktail

1 oz vanilla vodka
½ oz white rum
2 oz heavy cream
1 oz goat milk
¾ oz simple syrup (see page 137)
chocolate chips (garnish)
homemade whipped cream* (garnish)
confectioner's sugar (garnish)

Directions Add all ingredients in a mixing glass with ice. Shake well and strain into a metal martini glass. Garnish with whipped cream, 3 chocolate chips, and confectioners' sugar.

*Homemade whipped cream Chill a mixing bowl in the refrigerator 15–20 minutes prior to making your whipped cream. Add 1 cup heavy cream to the bowl and beat using an electric mixer until stiff peaks are about to form. Add 1 tablespoon of confectioners' sugar and 1 teaspoon vanilla extract and beat until peaks form. Do not overbeat, as lumps will form.

Tiramisu

THE ORIGIN OF TIRAMISU is highly debated. Some sources will tell you that it was first invented in the 1970s by a cook named Roberto Loli Linguanotto. Others will tell you that its origins date all the way back to 1800 in Treviso. Still others say that it originated in areas ranging from Siena to Piedmont and Veneto. One aspect of the dessert that is not as contested is what the main ingredients are: eggs, cocoa powder, coffee, sugar, mascarpone, and savoiardi, which is similar to a dry biscuit or ladyfinger. In fact, in official competitions, these six ingredients are required regardless of what tiramisu variations entrants want to make. The biscuits are dipped in the coffee, and the mascarpone, a soft, buttery Italian double cream cheese, is mixed with the eggs and sugar.

In its most common form, the word *tiramisu* means "pick me up" or "lift me up." *Tiramisu* is the fifth most recognized Italian word among Europeans, and it appears in the vocabulary of as many as twenty-three different languages. The dish is traditionally made in a round shape, but over time, the shape shifted into a square due to the limitations of the ladyfinger biscuits.

Making tiramisu involves layering the custard on top of the coffee and liquor-soaked biscuits. One of the great features of the dessert is the different play in textures, as the ladyfingers and custard complement each other to create a decadent yet still relatively light dessert. For the cocktail, I would suggest using a dark-roast coffee or espresso to really deliver the coffee flavor synonymous with tiramisu. I purchased freshly baked ladyfingers in the bakery at my local grocery store and have found that most stores carry them. Finish the cocktail with a light dusting of cocoa powder, and it's ready to serve!

Tiramisu: The Cocktail

1 oz aged rum
½ oz vanilla vodka
2 oz heavy cream
1 oz espresso or strong black coffee
¾ oz simple syrup (see page 137)
cocoa powder (garnish)
2 ladyfingers (garnish)

Directions Add ingredients to a mixing glass with ice. Shake well and strain into a large coupe glass. Garnish with 2 ladyfingers (still stuck together) and dust with cocoa powder using a fine mesh strainer.

Spain

Turrón

TURRÓN IS A SWEET TREAT made from a mixture of honey, eggs, sugar, and toasted nuts. The most common type of nut used in turrón is almonds, although other nuts such as pistachios can sometimes be used in place of almonds. This Spanish dessert is enjoyed throughout the year, but it is most popular during the Christmas season, when it is an essential component of any festive meal.

The most important distinction between types of turrón is whether it is hard and brittle or soft and chewy. The harder variety is known as *turrón duro* or *turrón de alicante*; the softer type is known as *turrón blando* or *turrón de jijona*. Rules strictly control whether a turrón may be labeled "suprema" or "extra." The top quality is "suprema," and to don that label, the soft turrón must contain at least 60 percent almonds, and the hard turrón must be 64 percent almonds. After that, there are "extra," "estándar" (standard), and "popular."

The Moors brought turrón to Europe, where it became popular, especially in Spain, France, and Italy. The Moors invaded Spain back in the early Middle Ages, and along with their architecture (such as Mudéjar art) and their language (the Arabic prefix *al-* is still present at the beginning of many Spanish words), they also brought with them a rich culinary heritage.

In 2010, the province of Alicante alone produced over fifteen million tons of turrón, 89 percent of which is sold around Christmastime. During the holiday season, it's not uncommon for turrón to be one of the many gifts "pooped" by the famous Caga Tío—a log that, when hit with a wooden stick on Christmas Eve, produces gifts to the astonishment of children. While modern methods of production have facilitated the process, much of Spain's turrón is still made according to traditional recipes and methods. The country is the biggest exporter of turrón in the world and primarily exports to South America but also to the Middle East and Japan, along with neighboring countries such as Germany and Italy.

Turrón is a delicious nougat confection that shines on the back of its base ingredient: almonds. The cocktail I created for turrón incorporates almonds in the form of amaretto, an Italian almond-flavored liqueur. Originally produced in Saronno, Italy, amaretto was formerly made with bitter almonds but is now generally produced with essences of apricot, peach, and cherry stones to source its flavoring. The cocktail's texture is lightened with the egg white and almond slivers, and a dusting of confectioners' sugar adds a final touch to the drink inspired by Spain's most popular sweet treat.

Turrón: The Cocktail

1½ oz vodka
¾ oz amaretto
½ oz freshly squeezed orange juice
¼ oz honey syrup (see page 136)
¼ oz lemon juice
1 egg white
confectioners' sugar
almond slivers (3, garnish)

Directions

Combine all ingredients and dry shake (no ice). Add ice, shake well, and strain into a coupe glass. Garnish with dusting of confectioners' sugar and 3 almond slivers.

Tarta de Manzana

TARTA DE MANZANA is a homemade traditional Spanish apple tart. Apple pie is a classic dessert, and of course Spain has its own version. Tarta de manzana is a classic pastry dessert served in many restaurants and patisserie shops across the Basque region of Spain. The origin of this dessert comes from neighboring France, and the adaptation of this classic French dessert in Basque patisserie shops during the late nineteenth century was a way of offering discerning clients quality Parisian products.

There are many variations on the recipe for tarta de manzana. Some recipes use shortcrust pastry, while others use puff pastry; some call for filling the tarte with apple compote, while others use pastry cream. That being said, there is an element to the dessert that all recipes agree on: a top layer of thinly sliced apples brushed with butter, baked in the oven until golden brown, and finished with a glaze of apricot jam.

Desserts are comforting, and no dessert may make you feel as warm and cozy as homemade apple pie. The tarta de manzana is Spain's version of this classic confection. I was excited to work on a cocktail for the tarta de manzana, as I love using freshly pressed juices, especially apple juice. The juice from the Granny Smith apples blends nicely with the apricot brandy and calvados, an apple brandy produced exclusively in Normandy, France. For the dessert to be classified as a true tarta de manzana, fresh apple slices must appear on top, and they appear on top of the cocktail, as well.

Tarta de Manzana: The Cocktail

2 oz calvados
1½ oz fresh Granny Smith apple juice
¾ oz apricot brandy
½ oz lemon juice
¼ oz simple syrup (see page 137)
3 apple slices (garnish)

Directions Add all ingredients in a mixing glass with ice. Shake well and strain into a large coupe glass. Garnish with apple slices arranged in a fan on a cocktail spear.

France

Éclair

AN ÉCLAIR IS AN OBLONG French treat made from choux pastry that is filled with cream or custard and dipped in fondant icing or ganache. Éclair means "lightning" in French, though no one knows why the term has been applied to this dessert. Some think it's because you often eat them lighting fast, or perhaps it is a reference to the gleam of light from the shiny fondant icing.

The choux pastry (*pâte à choux*) is a key component of the éclair. It is also used in making cream puffs, profiteroles, and gougères. This pastry rises only from the action of steam and does not include any yeast, baking powder, or baking soda. Pastry cream—a thick custard made with egg yolks, milk, sugar, cornstarch, and sometimes butter—is typically the filling. The most famous éclair is the chocolate one, and there is even a national day in France devoted to it on June 22.

Antonin Carême (1784–1833), one of the first celebrity chefs, is credited with making the éclair legendary by adding his magic touch to a cake previously known as *pain à la duchesse* or *petite duchesse*. Carême was the chef who baked Napoleon's wedding cake and created gastronomic masterpieces for the Prince de Talleyrand at the Chateau de Valençay. He was invited to cook for the Romanovs in St. Petersburg and made soufflés flecked with real gold for the wealthy Rothschilds in Paris. He became world famous for his cookbooks that were published in Paris. The éclair is revered in France, and you will find a version in every patisserie.

The éclair is by no means a light dessert. A dense custard or pastry cream fills the inside of the choux pastry, and it was important to create a cocktail that captures the creamy texture of the revered treat. To accomplish this, I used a whole egg in the cocktail. When using dairy, especially egg whites or whole eggs, it's important to dry shake using no ice prior to adding ice for the follow-up shake. The dry shake helps emulsify the egg and create a properly mixed cocktail.

Éclair: The Cocktail

1¼ oz vodka
¼ oz vanilla vodka
2 oz heavy cream
1 oz dulce de leche (see page 136)
¼ oz Lyons chocolate dessert sauce
1 whole egg
chocolate drizzle (garnish)

Directions Add all ingredients in a mixing glass and dry shake (no ice) for 15 seconds. Add ice and shake well. Strain into a coupe glass and garnish with chocolate drizzle in the shape of an éclair on top of the cocktail.

Crêpe

CRÊPE IS THE French word for pancake and differs from the traditional pancake in that it is lighter and thinner and can be used
in both sweet and savory dishes. Traditionally, buckwheat crêpes
are served with savory fillings, while the more delicately flavored
wheat crêpes are served with fruit and other sweet fillings. Their
name comes from the Old French *crespe*, which traces back to the
Latin *crispa* or *crispus*, meaning "curled"; this likely refers to their
often slightly ruffled edges. Whenever milk was in short supply
during the Middle Ages, adventurous crêpe lovers used a mixture
of wine and water as a substitute.

A French café that specializes in crêpes is known as a crêperie.
In Brittany, they still prefer crêpes made with local buckwheat
flour and use the slightly derisive *crêpes de froment* in reference
to crêpes made with white flour. A crêperie may be a take-out
restaurant or stall that serves crêpes as street food or a more
formal sit-down restaurant or café. Crêperies are typical of the
Brittany region of France, but they can be found throughout
France, Europe, and even Tokyo, the United States, and Canada.
In the Canadian province of Québec, crêperies are especially
abundant because of the French influence.

The history of crêpes dates back to thirteenth-century Brittany, France, when a housewife there accidentally dribbled some
thin porridge onto a hot, flat cooktop. It was not a period of time
to waste food, even after a cooking mistake, so she decided to
eat it. However, by far the most popular origin story of the crêpe
takes place at one of the tables of the Café de Paris in Monte
Carlo. The story goes that in 1895, fourteen-year-old Henri

Charpentier—the French chef who went on to become chef to John D. Rockefeller—created the dessert as a happy accident for the Prince of Wales while working in the kitchens of the renowned restaurant. The prince loved the flambéed crêpe with its zesty sauce and encouraged Charpentier to name the dish after one of his dining guests, a young French girl called Suzette—and voilà, crêpes suzette!

The crêpe has cemented itself around the world as a delicious savory or sweet treat. For our purposes, I chose to use the sweet dessert crêpe as a muse for the cocktail, which incorporates ripe banana, Nutella, raspberry liqueur, and Frangelico (for the hazelnut flavor)—ingredients and flavors associated with popular sweet crêpe varieties found across the globe.

Crêpe: The Cocktail

1½ oz Grey Goose vodka
¾ oz Frangelico
¾ oz Mathilde Framboise liqueur
1½ oz half-and-half cream
½ oz Nutella chocolate hazelnut spread
¼ ripe banana
Lyons chocolate sauce (garnish)
sliced bananas (garnish)

Directions Combine the vodka and banana in a mixing glass, muddling the banana until it resembles a puree. Add remaining ingredients with ice. Shake well and strain into a coupe glass. Garnish with sliced bananas on a cocktail spear drizzled with chocolate sauce.

Crème Brûlée

IT'S COMMON TO ASSUME that crème brûlée is a French dish. After all, the name is French and means "burnt cream." However, the name *crème brûlée* didn't become popular until the nineteenth century, and the dessert is probably just another version of a custard recipe that was passed around through the Middle Ages. The French version of this dessert is baked in a pan of water and chilled for several hours. The custard is sprinkled with sugar and then caramelized with a kitchen blowtorch and served quickly to preserve the contrast between the smooth, cold custard and crunchy, hot topping.

There are English recipes for something very similar to crème brûlée that date all the way back to the fifteenth century. During calving season in the spring in England, the milk was especially rich, and a sweetened custard was made seasonally to take advantage of those days. Some say the burnt sugar was added later at Trinity College in Cambridge, where a student is credited with the idea of branding the school crest into a topping of sugar; the creation is called *Cambridge cream* or *Trinity cream* and has been a staple on the school's menu ever since.

One figure who helped bring crème brûlée to the mainstream—prior to the dessert becoming a megahit among restaurants across the world—was Julia Child, an avid culinary and cultural figure who showed American audiences the art of making a crème brûlée on her television show, *The French Chef*.

Crème brûlée has to be atop the list of the most popular and celebrated desserts of all time. There is no mistaking a properly made crème brûlée, with its crisp caramelized sugar topping and rich custard filling. I have to admit I was excited to get the

blowtorch out for this cocktail. The idea is to get that same caramelized sugar on the rim of the glass as you would get on the top of your crème brûlée dessert. To give the cocktail the thick texture similar to the custard in crème brûlée, I use a whole egg, which again needs to be shaken without ice prior to chilling the drink down with ice.

Crème Brûlée: The Cocktail

1 oz vodka
¾ oz simple syrup (see page 137)
1½ oz heavy cream
½ oz vanilla vodka
1 whole egg
turbinado sugar (garnish)
cinnamon (garnish)
raspberries, blueberries (garnish)
mint (garnish)

Directions Combine all ingredients in a shaker and dry shake (no ice). Dip the rim of a coupe glass in cream, then line with turbinado sugar and cinnamon. Hold the glass upside down and heat the sugar and cinnamon with a small torch until the sugar begins to caramelize and turn brown. Add ice to the shaker, shake well, and strain into the coupe glass. Garnish with mint and then raspberries and blueberries on a cocktail spear.

Germany

Black Forest Cake

THE TRADITIONAL VERSION of Black Forest cake consists of multiple layers of chocolate sponge cake with whipped cream and cherries; it is covered on each side with whipped cream and chocolate chips and garnished with cherries on top. The bottom layers of sponge cake are also brushed with kirschwasser, or cherry schnapps, to provide moisture and extra flavor.

Many historians say that Black Forest cake dates back to the 1500s, when chocolate first became available in Europe. More specifically, its birthplace would have been the Black Forest region of Germany, which is known for its sour cherries and kirschwasser. The Schwarzwälder, or Black Forest, is a popular tourist destination in Germany, with dense forests and beautiful highlands. This region is known for its abundant and beautiful cherry trees; an early custom called for newlyweds to plant a cherry tree, which was said to be an inspiration for the creators of the cake.

Others argue that the cake bears the name *Black Forest* not because that is where it was invented but because it resembles

the Bollenhut costumes with red pom-poms that women use for traditional dances in that area. Still others say that the name is more metaphorical, with the cake evoking the dark, dense moisture of the shady forest.

Black Forest cake doesn't always make it to the table for traditional celebrations throughout the year, but when it does show up, it certainly stands out. Few confections are as visually stunning as the chocolate sponge cake with delicious cherry filling and a chocolate coating that resembles the forest of the region for which it was named. The main ingredients of the cocktail are chocolate and cherry, plain and simple. I garnished the inside of the coupe glass with chocolate flecks by dipping a toothpick in the chocolate sauce and applying it liberally, then finished the drink with Luxardo maraschino cherries to really give the cocktail the look of the Black Forest cake.

Black Forest Cake: The Cocktail

¾ oz aged rum

¾ oz chocolate vodka

¾ oz Godiva chocolate liqueur

2 oz heavy cream

¾ oz simple syrup (see page 137)

½ oz tart cherry juice

¼ oz kirsch

Lyons chocolate dessert sauce (garnish)

Luxardo maraschino cherries (garnish)

Directions Prior to mixing the drink, place a coupe glass in the freezer for about 10–15 minutes to chill, then dot the inside of the glass by using a toothpick with chocolate sauce on it. Next, combine all ingredients in a mixing glass with ice. Shake well and strain into a coupe glass. Garnish with 3 cherries on the rim of the glass.

United Kingdom

English Trifle

THE WORD *trifle* comes from the Old French term *trufle* and literally means "something whimsical or of little consequence." In essence, this means that making trifles should not be an arduous process; instead, it should be easy to assemble, serve, and eat the dessert. A proper English trifle is made with real egg custard poured over sponge cake soaked in fruit and sherry or brandy and topped with whipped cream. The trifle is typically served in glass dessert cups that show off its colorful layers. Recipes for trifles date as far back as the 1590s. Because the dessert is relatively easy to make, trifles are often made at home, especially at Christmas.

The first trifles were very much like fools (an old confection of pureed fruit mixed with cream), and the two terms were used almost interchangeably for years. Many puddings evolved as a way of using up leftovers. In fact, the trifle originated as a way to use stale cake. The English trifle is a close cousin of an Italian version called *zuppa inglese* (English soup) and is likely a distant relative to a Spanish dessert called *bizcocho borracho*.

The recipe for trifle—and many of its now-heirloom glass dishes—came to America via the British who settled in the coastal South. Its popularity gained traction from Southern planters who loved indulgent desserts. In the mid-1700s, cake (or biscuits), alcohol, and custard were combined in the trifle bowl. Supposedly, this dessert was called *tipsy parson* because it presumably lured many a Sunday-visiting preacher off the wagon. Southern hostesses prided themselves on their elegant table settings and considered a cut-glass trifle bowl to be mandatory for a properly presented trifle.

As a kid watching my mom work her magic in the kitchen, I was always fascinated when she made a trifle. I loved the formality of getting out the trifle bowl—the only time this particular vessel was ever used—and watching as the layers began to take shape. Cake, custard, and fruit—what's not to love? My goal was to create the trifle cocktail using the same elements that I loved as a kid, particularly the layering or wavy features of the dessert, which is achieved in this case with the raspberry sauce, along with the fresh strawberry slices and mint garnish.

English Trifle: The Cocktail

1½ oz Mathilde Framboise liqueur

1 oz aged rum

½ oz strawberry preserves

¼ oz cream sherry

¼ oz Frangelico

2 oz heavy cream

strawberry slices (garnish)

mint (garnish)

Lyons raspberry dessert sauce (garnish)

Directions Layer the inside of a goblet glass with raspberry syrup. Add all ingredients in a mixing glass with ice. Shake well and strain into a goblet. Garnish with thin strawberry slices on a cocktail spear and mint.

Figgy Pudding

FIGGY PUDDING IS A treat that neither contains figs nor is a pudding in the American sense. Traditionally made in the shape of a cannonball, figgy puddings, or Christmas puddings, are doused in alcohol—most often rum or brandy—to draw out and intensify the flavor.

Figgy pudding has a long history dating back to at least the seventeenth century. Beef and mutton were mixed with raisins and prunes, wines, and spices. When grains were added to make it a porridge, it was known as *frumenty*. In the early fifteenth century, it morphed into *plum pottage*. A mix of meats, vegetables, grains, fats, spices, and fruits—most notably raisins and currants, not actual plums—it was packaged like huge sausages in animal stomachs and intestines to be kept until it was served months later.

The dish that eventually evolved into plum pudding originally contained preserved, sweetened meat "pyes" and boiled "pottage," or vegetables, and was enjoyed in Britain as early as Roman times. By Elizabeth I's day, prunes had become popular, and the name became a portmanteau label for all dried fruits. As plums became synonymous with fruit, plum dishes with and without meat became party food.

By the end of the sixteenth century, fruit had become more plentiful, and plum pudding went from being savory to sweet. Around the same time, carolers began to sing the English folk song "We Wish You a Merry Christmas." When poor folks stood on the doorsteps of the wealthy and sang, "Oh, bring us some figgy pudding," and "We won't go until we get some," they were likely poking fun, albeit sarcastically, about the relationship between the two classes and spreading Christmas cheer.

Steamed plum puddings soon became highly anticipated Christmas treats that required lots of patience. By the nineteenth century, cooks traditionally gave their plum puddings at least a month to develop their signature spicy flavors. On Stir-up Sunday, the Sunday before Advent which falls five Sundays before Christmas, entire families would make their Christmas pudding. The namesake for the day wasn't derived from an actual need to stir up a pudding, but rather from a line traditionally read at church on Sunday.

It's nearly impossible to separate figgy pudding from Christmastime. They just go hand in hand, as the carolers of the late sixteenth century made clear when they regaled those who opened their front doors. It is interesting that figgy pudding is really not a pudding at all, at least as Americans tend to define the word. More cake than custard, figgy pudding is loaded with fresh fruits and, thankfully, brandy, which worked perfectly for the cocktail devoted to the holiday dessert. I included calvados, a brandy made from apples, to enhance the overall fruit flavor, while the egg white helps mimic the steamed cake texture of figgy pudding.

Figgy Pudding: The Cocktail

1 oz calvados
1 oz brandy
1½ oz fig simple syrup (see page 136)
½ oz freshly squeezed orange juice
¼ oz lemon juice
1 dash of allspice
1 egg white
mint (garnish)
dried cranberries (garnish)

Directions Add all ingredients in a mixing glass and dry shake (no ice) for 15 seconds to emulsify the egg white. Add ice, shake well, and strain into a coupe glass. Garnish with cranberries and mint on a cocktail spear.

chapter 4

Africa

Egypt

Lokma

okma is a sweet dessert consisting of deep-fried dough balls
dipped in honey syrup, rolled in sugar, and sprinkled with
cinnamon. Its origin can be traced to Egypt, Greece, and
Persia.

As early as the thirteenth century, historian Abd al-Latif al-
Baghdadi, a specialist in Egyptian culture, referred to these small
morsels covered with honey as *luqmat al-qadi* (judge's morsels).
Lokma is considered to be one of the oldest-recorded desserts
in the world. In ancient Greece, it was served to the winners of
the Greek Olympics. The Greek poet Callimachus was the first to
state that these deep-fried dough balls were soaked in honey and
then served to the winners as "honey tokens." This same recipe
spread all over the ancient world.

In Turkey, lokma is served without honey or any other sweetener. For centuries, it was prepared by the royal cooks of the
Ottoman Empire. The dessert has a ceremonial meaning and is
reserved for special occasions. Tradition states that forty days

after the death of an individual, family and friends gather to cook lokma and offer it to neighbors and pedestrians, who line up to receive the dessert and recite a prayer in honor of the soul of the deceased.

Although it is a simple dessert, lokma, similar to an American doughnut, is packed with delicious flavor and is made for special occasions. My goal was to create an easy-to-mix cocktail that packs a lot of flavor in just a few simple steps. The dashes of rose water add a nice floral component to the drink that balances the sweet and sour provided by the honey and fresh lemon juice.

Lokma: The Cocktail

2½ oz light rum
1 oz honey syrup (see page 136)
½ oz lemon juice
3 dashes of rose water
lemon twist (garnish)

Directions Add all ingredients in a mixing glass with ice. Shake well and strain into a coupe glass. Garnish with lemon twist.

Morocco

Seffa

SEFFA IS A traditional Moroccan dish that is typically reserved for celebrations and festivities. It consists of either vermicelli noodles or couscous combined with a savory-sweet onion sauce and a topping of icing sugar, cinnamon, raisins, and ground almonds.

The cuisine of Morocco is characterized by Berber, Moorish, and Arab influences and includes a large array of fruits and vegetables found on Mediterranean coastlines. Dishes in Morocco tend to be more spiced than others in the Middle East, and popular seasonings include turmeric, cinnamon, cumin, ginger, pepper, saffron, and paprika. Common meats used in Moroccan cooking are beef, mutton and lamb, chicken, camel, rabbit, and, of course, seafood.

Seffa is so beloved in the country that there are salty and sweet versions. This dish is usually served at the end of the main meal, before the dessert or as the dessert. Seffa is very simple to prepare and does not require a lot of time in the kitchen. It is usually made for special occasions, such as family gatherings, the birth of a baby, or weddings.

For the seffa cocktail, my goal was to highlight the almond flavor and spices present in the dish. Moroccan cuisine is unique in that cooks masterfully couple sweet and savory flavors—pairings you might initially think do not belong together. I was excited to incorporate almond milk and tawny port wine in the cocktail. I chose tawny over ruby port because of its nutty, caramel flavor, which it gets from being aged in small oak barrels.

Seffa: The Cocktail

2 oz amaretto
1 oz tawny port wine
2 oz almond milk
¼ oz lemon juice
2 dashes of cinnamon
lemon twist (garnish)

Directions Combine all ingredients in a mixing glass with ice. Shake well and strain into a coupe glass. Garnish with thick lemon twist.

Liquid Dessert

South Africa

Malva Pudding

MALVA PUDDING IS AN apricot-flavored cake-like dessert popular in the former Dutch colonies of South Africa. The dessert is baked and contains primarily egg yolks, butter, and apricot jam or preserves, resulting in a spongy, sweet, and moist pudding that is most often served with cream or vanilla ice cream. The moist, spongelike custard texture of malva pudding is why it's considered a pudding rather than a cake. In restaurants, the pudding is often prepared in individual baking dishes or ramekins, while at home, it is more common for the dessert to be cooked in round cake pans or loaf-sized baking dishes.

The origins of malva pudding are decidedly Dutch. Dutch colonists brought the pudding to South Africa when they arrived, most in connection with Dutch East India explorations, in the mid-1600s. The dessert provided a taste of home for European families who were establishing a colony in the hot and arid African climate.

The *Oxford English Dictionary* asserts that the name of the dessert comes from the Afrikaans term *malvalekker* (marshmallow). It is also believed to have ties to the Latin term *malva*, which refers to a mallow. Although there are no marshmallows actually used in the making of the dessert, the link is believed to have been derived from the pudding's texture, which is similar to that of a marshmallow. Another theory on the origin of the dessert's name comes from the belief that rose-scented malva leaves were either baked into the batter or boiled to create a liquid that would then be added to the sponge after it had been baked.

Malva pudding is popular today among all residents, both those native to South Africa and those of European descent. It is an important facet of South African dessert culture and is especially popular in South Africa's capital, Cape Town.

Malva pudding relies heavily on its infusion of apricot flavor and is commonly served à la mode. I found that mixing the cocktail with apricot brandy and vanilla vodka created a nice combination, especially when paired with heavy cream, a nod to the ice cream with which it is often served. A touch of fresh lemon juice helps cut the sweetness and adds a refreshing citrus note to the cocktail created in honor of one of South Africa's most popular desserts.

Malva Pudding: The Cocktail

1¼ oz vanilla vodka
1¼ oz apricot brandy
1½ oz heavy cream
1 oz brown sugar simple syrup (see page 135)
¼ oz lemon juice
lemon spiral (garnish)

Directions Combine all ingredients in a mixing glass with ice. Shake well and strain into a coupe glass. Garnish with lemon spiral.

chapter 5

Australia

Sydney

Pavlova

avlova is an airy dessert made from a crisp meringue shell topped with whipped cream and fruit. On Christmas Day, after the last prawn has been peeled, the white meringue cake is proudly displayed on tables across Australia. Pavlova is also synonymous with summer celebrations, as it's a refreshing sweet treat on hot and sticky days.

Australia and New Zealand have a sibling-like rivalry, arguing over sports, the nationality of Russell Crowe, and, of course, food, but there is no controversy bigger than that surrounding the origin of pavlova, which is the subject of one of the countries' longest-running disputes. While Kiwis have their own recipe, down under, pavlova has been named as quintessentially Australian and features a crunchier meringue with the classic topping of cream and passion fruit.

Supposedly invented at a hotel in Perth, the dessert was declared by a diner to be "as light as Pavlova," in reference to Russian ballerina Anna Pavlova, born in 1885; as a result, the chef named the dessert—you guessed it—pavlova. During Anna Pavlova's

time as a celebrity, many dishes throughout the world were named after her, including pavlova ice cream in America and frogs' legs à la pavlova in France. The earliest-known pavlova recipe published in Australia is dated 1926. Both New Zealand and Australia agree on the origin of the dessert's name.

Pavlova is a visually stunning dessert that surely draws attention whenever it is placed on display. The crispy baked meringue outer layer encircles a soft cake inside, and the treat is garnished with mixed berries and mint to add a nice color and freshness to the dessert. Given the importance of meringue and egg whites in pavlova, I created a cocktail that is a play on the famous Ramos gin fizz, a fantastic cocktail that was created in New Orleans and incorporates both lemon and lime juice, egg white, and cream. The drink is served in a collins or highball glass without ice. It is important to dry shake the ingredients to get that frothy texture we associate with any great fizz.

Pavlova: The Cocktail

1½ oz gin
1 oz Mathilde Framboise liqueur
½ oz lemon juice
½ oz lime juice
¾ oz half-and-half cream
¾ oz simple syrup (see page 137)
1 egg white
soda water (to top)
mint (garnish)
strawberries, kiwi, blueberries (garnish)
baked meringue* (garnish)

Directions Dry shake all ingredients, except the soda water. Add ice, shake well, and strain into a collins or highball glass. Top with soda and garnish with baked meringue, fruit, and mint on a cocktail spear.

*Baked meringue Preheat oven to 425 degrees.
Add 3 egg whites (at room temperature) to a mixing bowl.
Beat egg whites with an electric mixer until frothy.
Add ¼ teaspoon cream of tartar until soft peaks form.
Gradually beat in ¼ cup sugar, 1 tablespoon at a time, until sugar dissolves and stiff peaks form.
Place meringue on a parchment paper–lined baking sheet and bake until tops of meringue begin to brown, about 4–5 minutes.

Australia

Tasmania

Cherry Ripes

CHERRY RIPES ARE THE oldest chocolate bars to be manufactured in Australia; the bars—a combination of cherries, coconut, and dark chocolate—have a sweet flavor and a soft texture and can be used as a dessert ingredient to make mud cake, brownies, or cheesecake. The Cherry Ripe chocolate bar was introduced in 1924 by MacRobertson Chocolates, which was taken over by Cadbury in 1967. The original MacRobertson's Cherry Ripe logo was used on the wrapper until 2002, when it was redesigned. In 2013, Roy Morgan Research found it to be Australia's most popular chocolate bar. In 2015, the Cadbury factory in Ringwood, Victoria, processed forty million Cherry Ripe bars, with six tons of chocolate being produced every two hours.

The first use of *Cherry Ripe* as a name for a food in Australia was for a cake and then a biscuit. The cake was manufactured and sold by Australia's first biscuit company, founded in 1854 by Thomas Swallow (1823–1890). Within five years, Swallow had taken in Thomas Harris Ariell; their business became Swallow & Ariell.

The name for the chocolate bar was likely suggested by the title of a traditional song with lyrics that dates back to the seventeenth century. The song was a recurring theme in John Buchan's World War I spy novel, *Mr. Standfast* (1919). A British silent romance film called *Cherry Ripe* was released in 1921; it was based on an 1878 novel of the same title, written by Helen Mathers.

Chocolate, cherry, and coconut—there may not be a more delicious confectionary combination on Earth! The Australians certainly know how to make a fantastic candy bar, and my goal was to create a cocktail that highlights the aforementioned combination. I chose rum and brandy as the base, both of which lend a nice subtle sweetness and punch that complement the cherry, chocolate, and coconut flavor profile. Fresh lemon juice is important for this drink, as it serves to cut the sweetness and balance the cocktail in a way that enhances the star combination that has made the Cherry Ripe Australia's favorite dessert.

Cherry Ripe: The Cocktail

1 oz aged rum

1 oz brandy

1 oz Godiva dark chocolate liqueur

¾ oz Bordeaux maraschino cherry juice (from jar)

¾ oz cream of coconut

¼ oz lemon juice

Bordeaux maraschino cherries (garnish)

Directions   Combine all ingredients in a mixing glass with ice. Shake well and strain into a coupe glass. Garnish with Bordeaux maraschino cherries on a cocktail spear.

chapter 6

Asia

Thailand

Mango Sticky Rice

hailand has successfully positioned itself as a prominent gastronomic destination in Southeast Asia, and the simple yet delicious mango sticky rice is regarded as one of the country's most popular desserts. Mango sticky rice can be found in many places around Bangkok, from street-food stalls to the most traditional restaurants. Some of Bangkok's most exclusive hotels even offer the dish as part of their fabulous high-end Sunday brunches.

Although mangoes seem to be available in Thailand year-round, they are at their peak ripeness from April to June, when the mango flesh is bright, yellow, and juicy. *Nam dawk mai* and *ok long* are the favorite varieties of mangoes in Thailand, as they are known for being particularly sweet. Mangoes are the most popular fruit in the world and were first grown in India five thousand years ago. Legend says that Buddha sat under the cool shade of a mango tree to meditate.

Sticky rice is a type of rice grown mainly in Southeast and East Asia. Its proper name is *glutinous rice*; though it doesn't actually contain any gluten, it turns sticky after cooking. According to historians, the Chinese have domesticated rice for over ten thousand years through the wild species Oryza rufipogon in the Yangtze River valley, which then expanded to Southeast Asia. Today, Asian farmers provide approximately 90 percent of the world's rice supply, which makes rice one of the main agricultural products in the region. The Thai people, especially farmers, believe that there is a goddess of rice—Mae Phosop—who guards the rice plants and helps them to grow strong. The farmers hold ceremonies to worship the goddess at different stages of rice planting.

Some of the simplest culinary creations are actually the most delicious, which is certainly the case with mango sticky rice. The confectionary world improved upon simple rice by adding ripe mangoes to create a tasty dessert. Aged rum and mangoes pair fantastically, and I added Choya Yuzu, a smooth Japanese citrus liqueur, to the mix.

Mango Sticky Rice: The Cocktail

2 oz aged Jamaican rum
1½ oz mango nectar juice
¾ oz Japanese Choya Yuzu
¾ oz lime juice
½ oz brown sugar
simple syrup (see page 137)
lime wheel (garnish)

Directions Combine all ingredients in a mixing glass with ice. Shake well and strain over ice in a collins glass. Garnish with lime wheel on the rim of the glass.

Vietnam

Chè Chu

CHÈ CHUỐI IS A simple Vietnamese dessert consisting of tapioca pearls and sliced bananas or the small, ripe, and sweet plantain varieties usually found in Southeast Asia. The tapioca and bananas are combined with coconut cream or coconut milk, and the dish is often sweetened and sometimes flavored with pandan leaves. The dessert pudding is eaten slightly warmed or at room temperature due to the use of tapioca pearls, though it can also be served cold.

Chè chuối originated in the rural countryside of Vietnam, where bananas and coconuts are abundant. Cooks there use a type of banana called chuối sứ, which is available in some markets in the United States. You are likely to find the dessert sold in plastic cups at Vietnamese grocery stores, but chè chuối can also be made at home. In northern Vietnam, *chè* is also the word for the tea plant.

Chè chuối has gained popularity in Vietnam and around the world, establishing itself as one of the most popular street foods in Vietnam, especially in big cities such as Ho Chi Minh City,

Nha Trang, Danang, and Hanoi, largely because of its low price and great taste.

The success of this dessert—and subsequent cocktail—depends on the ripeness of the plantains or bananas you use to make the puree. When creating this cocktail, I jumped at the chance to match the banana, coconut, and cream flavors with the earthy, unique sweetness of cachaça. Vietnam is certainly on my bucket list of places to travel due to the country's unrivaled beauty and delicious street food.

Chè Chuối: The Cocktail

1½ oz cachaça
1½ oz heavy cream
1 oz ripe plantain puree
½ oz cream of coconut
¼ oz lime juice
2 dashes of black walnut bitters
halved banana (garnish)

Directions Combine all ingredients in a mixing glass with ice. Shake well (10–15 seconds to help thin the puree). Strain into a rocks glass and garnish with halved banana on a cocktail spear.

Dragon Fruit

DRAGON FRUIT comes from a fruit tree belonging to the cactus family, a group of dry tropical plants originating in the desert region of Mexico and Colombia. Dragon fruit was brought to Vietnam by the French in the nineteenth century. Known for its hardy pink skin and seed-speckled flesh, the fruit tastes like a mix between a kiwi and pear and is slightly crunchy. Dragon fruit season is from April to October, with the most fruit coming from May to August. The fruit is packed with natural antioxidants like betalains, which are actually a class of pigment—specifically red and yellow—that gives dragon fruit its vivid color.

There has been a surplus of dragon fruit in Vietnam, as the country shut down much of its trade with China due to the COVID-19 pandemic. In an effort to use up the excess fruit, Ho Chi Minh City–based chain ABC Bakery developed a new recipe for bright pink bread by replacing 60 percent of the water in the dough with dragon fruit smoothie. The bread was an instant sensation in Vietnam. Even as the chain quickly ramped up production to make twenty thousand loaves of dragon fruit bread a day, ABC Bakery said that it had been forced to limit customers to only purchasing five loaves at a time.

The economic value of dragon fruit in Vietnam has skyrocketed in the past decades. The fruit makes up 55 percent of the country's fruit export, and while a small portion—about 20 percent—of the dragon fruit grown in the country is sold domestically, the remaining 80 percent is sold internationally. In 2016, Vietnam earned US$895,000,000 from the export of dragon fruit. The main importer of Vietnamese dragon fruit is China, which accounts for over 90 percent, followed by the United States and Thailand, which make up approximately 2 percent. Because dragon fruit is so profitable in Vietnam, people who work in agricultural jobs receive higher wages than those who work in cities; due to this, the rural-to-urban immigration rate is low there.

Dragon fruit is hard to miss when you're walking down the produce aisle at your local grocery store. With its pink skin and green scales, it's easy to see how it got its catchy name. When I first tried the fruit, I was expecting overpowering sweetness, but dragon fruit has more of an earthy taste, which is why I included a bit of simple syrup in the cocktail. I don't make a lot of blended drinks, but the beverage devoted to dragon fruit called for it. After blending, pour the cocktail into a highball glass with no ice, then garnish with a lime and a slice of the dragon fruit, a tropical refresher that certainly deserves a spot on the rim of your glass.

Dragon Fruit: The Cocktail

¾ oz aged rum
¾ oz light rum
3 oz half-and-half cream
¾ oz sweetened condensed milk
½ dragon fruit (inside scooped out)
½ oz simple syrup (see page 137)
¼ oz lime juice
slice of dragon fruit (garnish)
lime wedge (garnish)

Directions Combine all ingredients in a blender with about 1 cup crushed ice. Puree and pour into a highball glass. Garnish with a slice of dragon fruit and lime.

China

Egg Tarts

WITH THEIR CUSTARD filling and flaky pastry crust, Cantonese egg tarts are a must-have when visiting a Hong Kong–style bakery. Egg tarts have a pie-like butter crust and a smooth yellow filling composed of evaporated milk, sugar, and eggs. Today, this is the standard small-portion, or dim sum, egg tart found in restaurants; the dessert's popularity has not diminished over the years.

Unlike some European custard tarts, such as Portugal's brûléed *pastel de nata* (their egg tart), the Hong Kong egg tart's history is not as well known. Some assume it has Portuguese origins because of its similar flaky crust to the *pastel de nata*, but it's believed that the *daan tat*, or "egg tart," is actually a variation of the British custard tart.

"If you look back at the history, the origin of the egg tart is from England," says chef Chan Chun-hung, head instructor for Cantonese cuisine at the Vocational Training Council's Chinese Culinary Institute. The dim sum chef, who has more than four decades of experience in Cantonese cuisine, says that the British first brought custard tarts to southern China in the 1920s, and local chefs then adapted the recipe before it was brought to Hong Kong after World War II.

Texture is key in creating the cocktail devoted to China's renowned egg tarts (*daan tat* in Cantonese). To achieve a silky smooth, bold texture, I use a whole egg and dry shake (no ice) to help emulsify the egg prior to adding ice. Because the cocktail is very rich, some might like a smaller portion in the dim sum tradition; in this case, I would recommend pouring the cocktail into two smaller coupes to share.

Egg Tarts: The Cocktail

1¼ oz vodka
¼ oz vanilla vodka
¾ oz condensed milk
¾ oz simple syrup (see page 137)
1 oz heavy cream
1 whole egg

Directions Dry shake (no ice) all ingredients for 15–20 seconds. Add ice and shake well. Strain into coupe glass. No garnish.

Philippines

Passion Fruit

PASSION FRUIT IS A nutritious tropical fruit that has gained popularity over the years, especially among the health conscious. Despite its small size, the fruit is rich in antioxidants, vitamins, and plant compounds that contribute to a healthy lifestyle. Though it's a tropical fruit, some varieties of passion fruit can survive in subtropical climates, which is why it is grown all over the world; crops can be found in Europe, Asia, Australia, and South and North America. The fruit is a pepo—a type of berry—and it is round to oval and yellow or dark purple at maturity; inside is a soft to firm juicy filling with numerous seeds. Passion fruit is both eaten and juiced, and its nectar is often added to other fruit drinks to enhance the aroma.

The passion fruit is so named because it is one of the many species of passion flower, the English translation of the Latin genus name *Passiflora*. In around 1700, it was named *flor das cinco chagas* (flower of the five wounds) by missionaries in Brazil as an educational aid to depict the crucifixion of Christ while they tried to convert the Indigenous inhabitants to Christianity.

Filipinos are blessed with an abundance of tropical fruits in the country, with hundreds of species of fruit available, most of them edible and many a vital part of the local food and culture. If you take a drive through the provinces, you will see miles of fruit plantations, many of which are considered exotic and valuable in other countries. In the Philippines, passion fruit is commonly sold in public markets and public schools. Some vendors sell the fruit with a straw to allow for sucking the juice and seeds from inside.

While passion fruit isn't especially remarkable from the out-side, its vibrant seeds and filling impress once the fruit is sliced open. When using tropical fruits in cocktails, I'm immediately drawn to rum and tequila. For the passion fruit cocktail, I add cachaça, which matches well with a blanco tequila. The spiciness of the bitters adds another level to the flavor profile, rounding out this cocktail that is perfect for sipping on those hot summer days—or the frigid winter nights, when a blast of the tropics is just what the doctor ordered.

Passion Fruit: The Cocktail

1½ oz blanco tequila

½ oz cachaça

1 oz passion fruit simple syrup (see page 137)

1 oz lime

2 dashes of Angostura bitters

lime twist (garnish)

Directions   Combine all ingredients in a mixing glass with ice. Shake and strain over 2 large square cubes in rounded rocks glass. Garnish with lime twist.

chapter 7

Antarctica

Cape Adare

Explorer Cake (Fruitcake)

Researchers discovered a 106-year-old untouched fruitcake in an old explorer hut in Antarctica in 2017; shockingly, it still looked and smelled good enough to eat. The cake was found in a tin in a building at Cape Adare, which was used by Captain Robert Scott's party of explorers during the Terra Nova expedition from 1910 to 1913 (a doomed expedition that led to the death of the captain and his team on their return from the South Pole).

Cape Adare is the most northeastern peninsula in Victoria Land, East Antarctica. The cake was made by Huntley and Palmers, a brand of fruitcake Scott enjoyed. The fruitcake still had its paper wrapping. "Finding such a perfectly preserved fruitcake among them was quite a surprise," Lizzie Meek, program manager for artifacts at the Antarctic Heritage Trust, said. "It's an ideal high-energy food for Antarctic conditions and is still a favorite item on modern day trips to the ice."[1]

1. Sean Rossman, "106-Year-Old Fruitcake Found in Antarctica 'Looked and Smelled Edible,'" *USA Today*, August 15, 2017, https://www.usatoday.com /story/news/nation-now/2017/08/15/106-year-old-fruit-cake-found -antarctica-looked-and-smelled-edible/569949001/.

There is an organization dedicated to procuring items found from early expeditions to Antarctica. The Trust is a New Zealand nonprofit that conserves artifacts left behind by famous Antarctic explorers such as Scott. Aside from the cake, the Trust recently retrieved about 1,500 artifacts found at two huts at Cape Adare. The pieces were taken to New Zealand and are kept in a lab at Canterbury Museum.

Captain James Ross discovered Cape Adare in January 1841 and named it after his friend the Viscount Adare (the title is derived from European nobility and Adare, Ireland). In January 1895, Norwegian explorers Henrik Bull and Carsten Borchgrevink reached Cape Adare aboard the ship *Antarctic* and collected geological specimens. This was the first documented landing in Antarctica. Borchgrevink led his own expedition in 1899 and returned to the cape, where he constructed two huts, the first human structures built in Antarctica. The expedition members wintered on the continent, and the survivors were picked up in January 1900. This was the first expedition party ever to spend a winter on the Antarctic continent. Studies suggest that Cape Adare was covered in ice during the last glacial period and deglaciated around 16,000 years ago. The results suggest that it took several thousand years for penguin colonies to form when iceless surfaces became available.

Antarctica is not the natural path the mind takes when talking culinary traditions, but Earth's southernmost continent has gained a reputation as the world's most efficient walk-in refrigerator after the 106-year-old fruitcake was found in pristine condition. The dessert, which tends to be associated with the holidays, is now a favorite among explorers and researchers of Antarctica. It was interesting to deconstruct the dessert and find that so many of the flavors work perfectly as a cocktail. The fruits, tea, sugar, and spices blend seamlessly to produce a drink that takes the edge off after a long day of exploring the coldest place on Earth—or as just a cocktail before dinner at home.

Explorer Cake (Fruitcake): The Cocktail

1½ oz calvados

¾ oz amaretto

1 oz black tea

¾ oz brown sugar simple syrup (see page 135)

¾ oz lemon juice

¾ oz pineapple juice

½ oz tart cherry juice

2 dashes of nutmeg

candied pineapples and cherries (garnish)

Directions Combine all ingredients in a mixing glass with ice. Shake well and strain into a goblet. Garnish with candied pineapples and cherries on a cocktail spear.

Recipes for Syrups

Baklava simple syrup Combine 1 cup granulated sugar with 1 cup water in a saucepan. Heat over medium heat until all sugar has dissolved. Add ½ cup shelled pistachios and ½ cup walnut pieces. Simmer, partially covered, for 15 minutes. Mash the nuts and strain using fine mesh sieve. Let cool prior to using.

Blueberry simple syrup Combine 1 cup water and 1 cup cane sugar in a saucepan and bring to a simmer. Continue to simmer and stir until all sugar has dissolved. Add 1 cup fresh blueberries and simmer until blueberries are soft enough to mash. Mash and strain through a fine mesh sieve. Let cool before using.

Brown sugar simple syrup Combine 1 cup water with 1 cup brown sugar in a medium saucepan over medium-high heat. Simmer for about 10 minutes, stirring, until sugar has fully dissolved. Let cool prior to using.

Brown sugar walnut simple syrup Add 1 cup water to 1 cup brown sugar in a saucepan over medium heat. Stir until incorporated, then add ½ pound of walnuts, simmering for 10 minutes. Strain and let cool prior to using.

Dulce de leche Stir together 4 cups milk, 1¼ cups sugar, and ¼ teaspoon baking soda in a 3- or 4-quart heavy saucepan. Bring to a boil, then reduce heat and simmer uncovered, stirring occasionally, until caramelized and thickened, about 1½ to 2 hours. (It is important to stir continuously as the milk caramelizes to avoid burning.) Stir in 1 teaspoon vanilla, then transfer to a bowl to cool. This recipe yields about 1½ cups.

Note: The recipe for dulce de leche is a bit labor intensive, as you need to continuously stir. I found that using sweetened condensed milk as a substitute will give you a very similar flavor (though not quite as rich) if you don't have the time to make traditional dulce de leche.

Fig simple syrup Combine 1 cup sugar with 1 cup water in a medium saucepan. Heat over medium heat and stir until sugar has dissolved. Reduce heat and add ½ cup dried figs, ½ cup diced Granny Smith apples, 1 lemon peel, and 1 orange peel. Simmer, partially covered, for 15 minutes. Mash the fruit and strain using a fine mesh sieve. Let cool prior to using.

Honey syrup Combine 2 parts honey with 1 part warm water. Stir until honey thins to a syrup. Let cool prior to using.

Kataifi simple syrup Combine 1 cup water with 1 cup granulated sugar in a saucepan and heat on medium heat. Add 1 cup walnuts, 1 teaspoon honey, ½ teaspoon cinnamon, 1 lemon peel, and ¼ teaspoon ground cloves. Stir over medium-low heat for 10 minutes. While the syrup is still warm, mash the walnuts, then strain using a double strainer. Let cool prior to using.

Passion fruit simple syrup In a medium saucepan, combine 1 cup sugar with 1 cup water. Heat and stir until sugar is incorporated. Cut 4–5 passion fruits in half, scoop out inside, and add to the saucepan. Simmer over medium-low heat for 10 minutes. Strain using a fine mesh sieve. Let cool prior to using.

Simple syrup Combine 1 cup water with 1 cup sugar and simmer in a medium saucepan until a syrup forms. Let cool prior to using.

Sweet potato simple syrup Parboil 1 cubed sweet potato for 10 minutes, until soft. In a separate saucepan, mix 1 cup water with 1 cup sugar. Heat over medium-high heat and stir until sugar has dissolved. Add 1 cup parboiled sweet potatoes and simmer, partially covered, for 10 minutes. Mash sweet potatoes and strain through a fine mesh strainer. Let cool prior to using.

Bryan Paiement grew up in Roanoke, Virginia. He discovered his passion for creating cocktails in his late twenties and has been mixing ever since! He currently bartends and teaches cocktail classes at Ginger and Baker in Fort Collins, Colorado. Bryan is the author of two previous books, *Sports Bar: Cocktails and Sports Trivia* and *The Little Book of Whiskey Cocktails*. He lives in Fort Collins with his wife, Dana, son, Bodie, and their newest addition, Lily.

FOR INDIANA UNIVERSITY PRESS

Tony Brewer, *Artist and Book Designer*

Brian Carroll, *Rights Manager*

Samantha Heffner, *Trade Acquisitions Assistant*

Brenna Hosman, *Production Coordinator*

Katie Huggins, *Production Manager*

Dave Hulsey, *Acquisitions Editor and Director of Sales and Marketing*

Darja Malcolm-Clarke, *Project Manager and Editor*

Dan Pyle, *Online Publishing Manager*

Pamela Rude, *Senior Artist and Book Designer*

Stephen Williams, *Marketing and Publicity Manager*